Map Artwork Copyright © 2005 by Collan Kneale

Fig Tree Lane

British Cemetery Road

Back Road

Howard Street

Highway 12

School Road

Drive

Road

Hatteras Inlet Station

5

59

Parking
k to Beach
13.4

© Collan Kneale

One Boat Guides

Ocracoke Island

Walking Tour & Guidebook

One Boat Guides

Ocracoke
Island
Walking Tour & Guidebook

by Jenny Scarborough

FOURTH EDITION

Published by Narayana, Inc.
DBA One Boat Guides
Michael McOwen, Publisher
P.O. Box 308
Manteo, NC 27954

(252) 202-5548
e-mail: Michael@OneBoatGuides.com

4th Edition
1st Printing

Walking Tour Map & Ocracoke Island Map
Base Artwork Copyright © 2005
by Collan Kneale

Printed in the United States of America

ISBN 0-9768164-2-3

Table of Contents ❧

Post Card Courtesy: Michael G. Tames

SHRIMP BOAT and RIG in OCRACOKE HARBOR, OCRACOKE, N.C.
U.S. COAST GUARD STATION BACKGROUND

Acknowledgments vi

Introduction vii

Ocracoke Island Then xi

Ocracoke Walking Tour 1

Ocracoke Island Now 59

Ocracoke Island Weddings 64

Attractions 67

Recreation 73

Shopping 86

Restaurants 97

Accommodations 105

Acknowledgments

As with raising children, a book like this can not be created without the efforts and support of the whole community. The merits of this book are a direct result of the wonderful collaborative spirit that exists on Ocracoke.

I would like to thank the people of the Ocracoke Preservation Society once again for their incredible support with information, photographs and time spent helping pull together details. Linda Scarborough and Julie Howard dove right in whenever needed. Many thanks to you. And Janie Jacoby, Kris Weeks and Sally Newell should also be acknowledged.

I would also like to thank the many people who opened their family albums, told stories and allowed us to record some of their family history. In particular, thank you to Jim Wynn, Lanie Wynn, Clayton Gaskill, Philip Howard, Al Scarborough, Marlene Mathews, Bertha O'Neal, Larry Williams, Ann Warner, Susie Scott O'Neal, Debbie Wells, Ward and Linda Garrish, Sally Newell, Steve and Mary Wright, Sue Reed, Betty Helen

Chamberlin, Mickey Garrish O'Neal and Merle Smith Davis.

Thanks also to Michael G. Tames for preserving Outer Banks history by collecting old post cards and for allowing us to publish a few of them.

And special thanks to Ann Ehringhaus for encouragement from beginning to end and the tangible support with photos and information.

Everyone who reads this book will know about Jenny Scarborough's talents, but her wonderful spirit, enthusiasm and great humor are appreciated. Thank you for everything, Jenny.

Once again, Jenny Scarborough was in charge of the guidebook section in addition to the walking tour, but Molly Harrision's role as the original guidebook writer should not be overlooked. Thanks for the great foundation Molly.

And finally, thanks to Beth Storie, my wife and great friend who also happens to be an incredible editor and a blessing to everyone who has the good fortunate to spend time with her. — M.M.

Introduction ✦

Welcome to Ocracoke Island! The character of an island community 24 miles offshore can differ dramatically from that of a mainland town, and the observation has been made that no one feels ambivalent about Ocracoke. This book will be your personal guide to this unique and enchanting town. As you walk or bike along the route, we'll point out sites and homes of interest, share old photos, tell stories connecting families who have lived here since the days of piracy and fill you in on significant historic events. We'll also provide the inside scoop on all the dining, shopping, accommodations and attractions to be found.

Mrs. Bragg, also seen on the cover, was once the primary heath care provider for the island. This photo was taken in the 1960s.

Photo Courtesy: Ocracoke Preservation Society

The Ocracoke Walking Tour

The Walking Tour winds through the Historic District, along streets that were once sandy footpaths. Businesses and homes intermingle throughout the district. Picket fences, grave plots and sandy yards with oleander, scrub pine, red cedar, yaupon and black myrtle are traditionally found on old family lots. You'll also pass fish houses, docks, boats, the lighthouse, ancient live oaks, cemeteries, old cisterns and graciously tended gardens. Depending on the time of the year you will see nets being mended, stacks of crab pots or boats hauled for maintenance. While the 1.7 mile tour can be leisurely done in two hours, don't hesitate

Ocracoke In the 1960s.

Post Card Courtesy: Michael G. Tames

A Day's Catch of Channel Bass
Ocracoke, N. C.

32370

to diverge from the route, visit a working artist's studio or fine craft shop, eat locally caught and prepared seafood or pause to overhear locals swapping tales over coffee. After all, one of the great pleasures of Ocracoke is having little to do. Imagine you are visiting before 1942, when the U.S. Navy established a base on the island and paved the first road. (It is said two cars then promptly collided.) Envision banker ponies roaming freely, and people sharing news over picket fences or while sipping iced tea in porch rockers.

But don't lose yourself entirely in a romanticized past! Say hello to the people you see, and notice the ways islanders have adapted their property and buildings to modern uses. Because trees and lumber were traditionally scarce on Ocracoke, wood was valued and reused; a number of structures on the island have been relocated or contain timber salvaged from shipwrecks. This ethic continues today. Outbuildings on Ocracoke include an old morgue, retired wheelhouses and the odd rusting utility van. Many people opt to renovate or enlarge an existing building rather than raze and rebuild, all of which makes for spaces with a funky charm.

While you're pausing to admire the sites and other homes along the tour, please respect the privacy of the homeowners by not entering the property or bothering the residents. But people are proud of their homes, land, and history, so don't be shy about looking. This guide will enhance your knowledge of the island and serve as a reference to you when you're in the village, but we can't possibly include all the history and stories Ocracoke holds. There are several fine books about the island, which can be found in local shops. Happy touring. 🌶

Ocracoke Island Then

A common question from first-time visitors is "How do you pronounce the name of this place?" It seems people have been asking that for years. The earliest record of the island's name, on a map made by English explorer John White in 1585, designates the inlet as "Wokokon." Subsequent spellings include "Woccocock," "Oakacock" and "Okercock." The name derives from the Woccon tribe of Native Americans, who lived in the mainland tidewater and came to the island for seafood feasts in clement weather. The inlet, the island and the village now all carry the name Ocracoke, which, incidentally, is pronounced like the vegetable and the soft drink.

One of the expeditions Sir Walter Raleigh made between 1584 and 1587 landed here, and in 1715, a little more than a century after Jamestown was settled, the North Carolinan colonial assembly saw fit to pass an act placing pilots on the island. Many colonists lamented the hazards of the changing shoals of Ocracoke inlet, and the first residents guided boats over the shallow bar. The isolated inlet was also prone to smuggling. One man in particular was comfortable navigating the waters of Pamlico Sound, and in 1718 Edward Teach, or Blackbeard, was caught and beheaded as he and his ship hid in waters behind the island. After the pirate's death, people were more willing to settle, and by the time of the first census in 1790, 135 whites, two free

Photo Courtesy: Larry Williams

persons of color and 31 slaves lived on Ocracoke. There were 23 households and nine family names, most of which remain prominent: Bragg, Garrish, Gaskins, Howard, Jackson, Neale (in the 1800 census amended to O'Neal), Salter, Scarborough and Williams.

Early settlers kept livestock, fished and grew vegetables. The men piloted locally or worked on merchant ships travelling routes from New York to the West Indies. Through

Post Card Courtesy: Michael G. Tames

Small Herds of WILD PONIES still range the Outer Banks at OCRACOKE, N.C.

the Revolutionary and Civil wars remarkably little seems to have changed. During the Revolutionary War the shifting sands that had confounded early settlers enabled seafarers to foil the British Blockade. During the Civil War the Outer Banks quickly fell to Union Troops. Apparently islanders went about business as usual in spite of the occupying army. By 1860 the island was able to support several grocers and carpenters. Although the majority of men remained seafarers, more and more had begun fishing for a living, and some worked for the U.S. Lifesaving Service.

The Woccon Indians, who once came to indulge during the summer, were trendsetters of a sort. In the later 1800s wealthy mainland families began fleeing the marshy tidewater to summer on the island, and guided hunting and fishing

trips gained popularity as vacations. The development of steam power had diminished Ocracoke's importance as a port, and islanders adapted their skills to the changing economy. Though there was fledgling tourism, a clam processing plant on the island had closed, and the 1920s and 1930s saw an exodus of people to the ports of Newport News and Philadelphia, where jobs were more abundant.

After World War II, a growing middle class found its way to Ocracoke. The Navy had paved the first road and deepened Cockle Creek, which was given the more picturesque name of Silver Lake. More changes took place in the second half of the 20th century than at any other time in the island's settled history. Throughout the 1950s the village's roads were gradually paved. A National Park Service Seashore was established in 1953, including everything but the 775 acres of village on the northwest side of the island. Prior to 1956 all telephone calls had to be made or received at the Coast Guard Station. In 1957 North Carolina bought the four-car ferry that Mr. Frazier Peele ran between Ocracoke and Hattteras, and in the early 1960s the state purchased the vessel *Sea Level*, which traveled the Cedar Island route. In 1977 a water system provided an

Access onto the ferry has changed over the years.

alternative to cisterns and hand pumps. Tourism now dominates the economy, and each year the number of visitors increases.

Despite all this rapid change, Ocracoke continues to enchant, as much for its populace as for its natural beauty. Many natives still speak with a distinctive brogue, or dialect, and Ocracokers know how to tell a story. It's a necessary skill: The year round population is at an all-time high of about 760, winters can be full of chilly nor'easters and diversions many take for granted don't exist here. Though Ocracoke is an insular community, Ocracokers themselves are warmly generous and welcome sincere interest in their lives.

The island has wide sandy beaches with clean blue water, making it the perfect spot to throw out a fishing line or dig your feet in the sand or read a book. A stroll from one end of the village to the other takes perhaps 30 minutes, and bicycles are the ideal transportation. Kids can sign up for surfing lessons or safely explore the village on their own. Kayaking the sounds or wandering the national park makes for great birding and shelling. One can rake for clams then steam them on a beach fire. You can charter a boat and head offshore after the big one. Or you can just meander around town, visiting the distinct shops and galleries. (Go ahead, take a picture of yourself in front of the lighthouse.) On Ocracoke, it's okay to have a nap in a hammock, a cold beer in the middle of a hot day, or both. At sunset you can sail past Teach's Hole before dining on fresh seafood.

After a few days on the island, you're likely to recognize some faces. At the post office you might bump into the person who served you dinner, or you may strike up a conversation with a local shopkeeper over a morning bagel. Ocracoke *is* a small town. This guide will introduce you to the neighborhood, even if you are only on the island for a short time. 𝓔

Ocracoke Walking Tour ✿

1. David Williams House / Ocracoke Preservation Society Museum

This foursquare home with a steep hipped roof was built for David and Alice Wahab Williams, who lived here with their six children. Captain Williams was the first Chief of the U.S. Life Saving Station. His wife was the sister of James Hatton Wahab (Site #6). The Williams' were married in 1884 though the property was not deeded to them until 1890. It was customary to transfer title after a home had been built, and estimates for the building's age range from 1889 to 1900. Originally located near the Anchorage Inn, the house was surrounded by two fences, the larger of which enclosed horses and cattle. The gate to the inner fence opened outward to prevent livestock from grazing on the plants in yard.

In 1989 the home was moved to its present location by the Ocracoke Preservation Society to Prevent its demolition. The next year it opened as an historic house museum. The home is furnished with pieces from the 1930s and 1940s and includes maritime relics, decoys by native carvers, a display of local shells, artifacts from a now-submerged Civil War fort, a video presentation of the Ocracoke dialect and a small gift shop. The museum is free to the public though donations are encouraged.

Directions:
Take Highway 12 south to the Cedar Island/Swan Quarter ferry terminal. Park in the large lot across the street from the public docks. The tour begins at the David Williams house, which is to your right as you enter the parking lot.

Photo Credit: Ann Ehringhaus

The David Williams House before it was moved to its current location. This photo was taken just after Hurricane Gloria in 1985.

Directions:
Near the site of the current Coast Guard Station

Featured Attraction
• Ocracoke Preservations Society Museum .... page 69

2. Site of Grand Ponder Inn

First opened in 1885, the Grand Ponder or "Ponzer" Hotel was developed by a group of businessmen from mainland eastern North Carolina. Located near the present-day Coast Guard station, the hotel overlooked Pamlico Sound, with porches wrapping around the upper and lower stories of the cross-shaped building. Enlarged to 48 rooms after its first year of operation, it was a bustling place in the summertime. Steamers arrived from Washington, NC, and New Bern, and a horse-drawn trolley took guests

The Grand Ponder Inn before it was destroyed by fire.

to the beach.

In 1899 several dozen people rode out the "Old August Storm" in the dining room. The building sustained a good deal of damage, including the loss of the upstairs verandah roof. Some speculate the owners didn't want to bear the expense of repairs; others claim it was merely human foible that ultimately destroyed the Grand Ponder. The Credle brothers of Hyde County and New Bern were the last proprietors. In the spring of 1900 a boat captain and one of the brothers were cooking a goose on a Wilson heater. Realizing they had no pepper, the men went to the boat, and in their absence the pot boiled over.

By the time they returned the resulting fire was out of control, and the hotel burned to the ground.

3. Naval Station Site

This large cistern is a remnant of a WWII Navy Section Base established in 1942 to combat German submarine warfare, which targeted East Coast shipping lanes. In the first six months of that year, more than 60 ships were attacked and lost off the Outer Banks, earning it the name "Torpedo Junction." Islanders remember seeing the ocean burning and bodies covered with tar and oil washing ashore or into fishing nets. Residents were under blackout restrictions, and there were rumors, apparently unfounded, of spies staying on the island.

Several island men left as sailors and returned because of U-boat attacks. Artis Bryant was in the Merchant Marines during the Second World War. His freighter was torpedoed, and the lifeboat landed on Ocracoke. That night he was able to visit his family for the first time since about 1916. A sadder story is that of James Baugham Gaskill, who was an officer in the Merchant Marines. On March 11, 1942, his vessel, *Caribsea,* was southeast of Ocracoke. Hit by two torpedoes she sank within 20 minutes. Her distress signal was picked up, and local men spent the following days checking the surf for wreckage. His brother found debris containing Jim Baugham's Second Mate's license, and a piece of timber inscribed with "Caribsea" was made into a cross that stands in the Methodist Church. Jim Baum's body was never recovered.

The Navy successfully thwarted U-boat attacks toward the end of 1942, and the base was turned into a training facility. They paved roads and dredged the harbor to allow deep-draft access.

Directions:

Look across the parking lot and locate the flag pole. You'll see the old cistern of the Naval Base. You see the same cistern in the photo on the next page.

Note:

There are public restrooms at the Park Service Visitor Center by the flag pole. With the exception of facilities located in restaurants and shops these will be the only public restrooms on the walking tour.

The Cistern in 1979.

Photo Credit: Ann Ehringhaus

Pamlico Sound

Old C. G. Building
Barracks
Dispensary
Mess Hall & Galley
Administration
Movie Theater
Thaddeus & Polly Scarborough
Docks
Cistern
Radar Jamming Equipment
Garage & Machine Shops
George & Anna Bell O'Neal
Guard House

During World War II the Navy occupied all of the land between where the Coast Guard Station and the David Williams House are presently located.

Commissioning exercise at the Naval Base, September 5, 1944.

Many sailors boarded with locals, and several married island women and settled here. However, those who found romance were the exception. Being stationed on Ocracoke or putting into port here was considered a hardship. According to old Navy records, this was "due to the isolated position of the base, the poverty of entertainment of any kind, no liquor, and a lack of supply of the ladies of negotiable affections sought by sailors."

After the base was abandoned in 1945 most of the buildings were moved and used as hunting camps, cottages or additions to existing homes. On an island where disposable income was in short supply, other goods were quickly distributed as well. The property is currently administered by the National Park Service and the NC Department of Transportation and still known locally as "down base."

4. Berkley Manor

Since the early 1950s the Berkley Manor's four story tower has enhanced Silver Lake's skyline. Sam Jones, a Hyde County native and Norfolk industrialist, remodeled the Dezzie Fulcher home to entertain customers. His invitations to guests describe it as "a place of contentment and rest where the 'weak grow strong and the strong grow great.'" A 1954 visitor described a "mansion of some 20 rooms, furnished with an assortment of individually incongruous but upon the whole amazingly harmonious pieces of classic and modern art and furniture."

Jones built another island landmark, the Berkley Castle, as well as a Whittlers' Club for men, and a private residence. His love for Ocracoke and his extravagant and eccentric building habit created a boon for local builders. According to an early reporter, "Ocracoke local gossip has it that Sam Jones is his own architect and when he starts a building even he doesn't know what it will look like when it is finished." (A sidebar on Sam Jones is on page 48).

Directions:
From the David Williams House walk south (in the direction of the lighthouse). You'll see the Berkley Manor on your left.

Photo Credit: Ann Ehringhaus

A view of the Berkley Manor from the back side.

A view of a 1950 pony penning taken from the lawn of the Berkley Center. Silver Lake and the road that is now Highway 12 are in the background.

Directions:

Look across the harbor to spot the square two-story building on a pier.

The lawns have been used for local festivals and an occasional wedding; one Halloween the entire building was turned into a haunted house. The Jones family sold the property, and between the 1980s and 2004 the Berkley Manor was operated as an Inn.

5. Sam Jones Dock House

In the early 1900s similar structures surrounded the harbor. Water and wind have destroyed the majority of these buildings, yet fishermen still pull up with the day's catch at one of the two remaining commercial fish houses. This recently restored dock house belonged to Owen Gaskill in the 1940s. The interior was one room with high ceilings that created space to store fish boxes and seafood. At that time the building had a door on each side. A local man remembers shrimp being unloaded into the upper part of the building and spilling out the doors. He and other boys would sit on the docks amidst piles of shrimp and earn money for removing the heads.

Gaskill sold the building to Sam Jones in the 1950s, and Jones had an upstairs floor added. Some people say the wood used to build the interior staircase was once part of a home belonging to General George MacArthur. The dock house remains in the Jones family.

6. James Hatton Wahab House

This gabled home with a gracious lawn was built about 1887 for James Hatton and Martha Ann Howard Wahab. He was a member of the U.S. Life Saving Service. Their son Robert Stanley Wahab was born in 1888 and became one of Ocracoke's most prominent citizens. Stanley attended college in Wilmington, Delaware, and returned briefly to teach on the island. Though jobs kept him away for a time, he maintained his home here, and his vision and work are responsible for much of the modernization that took place before his death in 1967.

In the early 1900s Ocracoke was a poor place indeed. Ann Scarborough married an island man and first visited in the 1930s. She recalls, "'Course people didn't make no money, but it didn't cost much to live. They had gardens, cows, pigs. No one knew what a loaf of bread was. Everybody made their own biscuits every day." Having lived away from the island, Stanley Wahab recognized both the poverty and Ocracoke's potential as a resort. He ran Ocracoke's first moving picture show and brought the first car to the island in 1914. He encouraged the dredging of Cockle Creek in the 1930s and renamed it Silver Lake. He was largely responsible for the first electric and ice plant in 1936. Around this time he began building the Wahab Village Hotel and Theater (now Blackbeard's Lodge) to attract visitors to the island. He started a flying service between Manteo and Ocracoke in 1939, and he helped bring private phone lines in 1956. Wahab invested in the first ferry to Hatteras,

Directions:

Site 6 is next to the Berkley Center on your left.

Photo Courtesy: Larry Williams

An old tin type photograph of James Hatton Wahab (1861-1913).

Sidenotes ❧

Banker Ponies

The first European inhabitants of the island may have swum ashore after being tossed overboard in order to lighten a vessel's load. They found fresh water by stomping the ground and subsisted by eating tough marsh grasses. In the summer these horses avoided the mosquitoes and heat by wading into the

Photo Courtesy: Ocracoke Preservation Society

Bobby on the left is riding Little Teach and Lindsay Howard on the right is riding Old Teach.

sound. Though their origin is not known with certainty, it has been determined conclusively that the Banker ponies are of Spanish ancestry. These horses with a sloped croup and one fewer lumbar vertebra are small and hardy, earning them the inaccurate title of ponies.

By the early 1900s the herd numbered between 150 and 200. Though they roamed freely until 1957, they had owners and some were tamed for riding, hauling and plowing. Some men even

Photo Courtesy: Ocracoke Preservation Society

The ponies once roamed freely on the island (1950s photo).

hunted from horseback because wildfowl allowed a close approach (the ponies first had to be trained to not startle at the gunshot). One of the reasons island homes traditionally have picket fences was to keep wandering ponies from eating shrubbery in the yard. Horses that were ridden would simply come when called.

In the 1950s Ocracoke was home to the nation's only mounted Boy Scout troop. Each boy bought, caught and broke his own horse. Riding barefoot and bareback, the troop participated in rounding up cattle twice a year and the annual July 4th pennings. Men and boys spent the night in camps on the northern end of the island and began herding the animals around 4:30 or 5:00 a.m. By late morning the corrals were full, and the gelding, branding and breaking of the ponies went on into the evening. Bravado increased (and skill, perhaps, diminished) as many partook of homemade meal wine. The pony pennings were one of the year's largest social events.

The herd now numbers about two dozen, and the stock is kept fresh through interbreeding with other coastal herds and Spanish mustangs. Penned after Highway 12 was paved, the Park Service is responsible for the care of the horses. 🐾

Photo Courtesy: Ocracoke Preservation Society

The mounted Boy Scouts on the beach.

Photo Courtesy: Larry Williams

The Wahab House, picture taken after the 1937 addition of the sun porches on each side.

Directions:

Take an immediate left after the Anchorage Inn on to British Cemetery Rd. Site 7 is on the left just past Island Artworks.

abetted the establishment of a route between Ocracoke and Cedar Island and was vital in convincing the state to take over ferry operations. He would be pleased that Ocracokers now have some control of their economic destiny, and no longer have to be cold in the winter, hot in the summer and eat fish three meals a day.

7. Gillis Riddick House

The National Register of Historic Places calls this home "one of the finest bungalows on Ocracoke." The intact original ornamentation includes Japanese-influenced brackets at the eaves and beneath the front dormer. The porches' wide columns and solid rail are also noteworthy. Originally built by Thad Gaskins for Gillis Riddick around 1936, some of the wood came from the schooner *Nomis,* which wrecked in 1935. Robert Wahab and Elizabeth O'Neal Howard purchased the house in 1942. Wahab worked as an electrician for the Navy and was stationed at the base on Ocracoke. After leaving the service he managed the first electric plant and later worked as a plumber, electrician, carpenter and mason. Elizabeth was the island's

Photo Courtesy: Betty Helen Chamberlin

An early photo of the Gillis Riddick House.

postmistress for many years, a repository of
island lore, a
grand and
beloved lady, an
occasional
mischief-maker
and baker of the
world's finest
jelly cakes. The
home now
belongs to their
daughter, Betty
Helen
Chamberlin, an
island business-
woman.

Photo Courtesy: Ocracoke Preservation Society

The out-
building at the
end of the
driveway was
originally the
detached kitchen
of the U.S. Life
Saving Service and dates to the early 20th century.
During WWII it was used to hold the bodies of
British sailors who washed ashore after their
vessel was sunk by a torpedo.

8. Amasa Fulcher House

This home was originally a story and a jump
built around 1904 for Amasa "Mr. Mace" Fulcher
(1876-1946), who bought the property from his
grandfather for "$10 and natural love and
affection." Mr. Mace was an entrepreneur who in
1918 established the waterfront grocery that
preceded the Community Store. When the
bodies of four British seamen washed up during
World War II, it was Mr. Mace, a prominent
layman of the Methodist Church, who delivered
the rites. His daughter Fannie Pearl Fulcher
(1908-1997) corresponded with the widow of
one of the sailors and in 1952 visited her in
Britain.

*A view in the 1930s looking down
what is now British Cemetery
Road. The store in the foreground
was replaced by the first house
you'll see today on the right. The
second building, which is now
Over the Moon, was built in the
1870s for the O'Neal family.*

Directions:
Stay on British Cemetery Road.
Site 8 is the next house on your
left.

Fannie Pearl received her master's degree from Columbia University and was a career teacher in North Carolina schools. She summered on the island until her death. Her niece and nephew now own the home and maintain it much as she did.

The Community Store around the 1950s.

The kitchen's running water is still in an attached room, and several of Fannie Pearl's oil paintings grace the walls.

Directions:

The British Cemetery will be on the right immediately after you pass Teeters's Campground.

9. British Cemetery

The H.M.S. *Bedfordshire* was a British commercial fishing trawler built in 1935 and re-fitted for anti-submarine warfare at the outbreak of World War II. When German U-boats began to devastate East Coast shipping in early 1942, a crew of four officers and 33 men left Britain aboard the

Bedfordshire to help their American allies. The vessel patrolled between Cape Lookout and Norfolk, escorting convoys and aiding ships that had been torpedoed.

In April she put ashore at the Naval Base in Norfolk, Virginia. Lt. Thomas Cunningham and another officer happened to meet and dine with Robert Wahab Howard of Ocracoke (Site #6). A short time later the *Bedfordshire* journeyed south and docked in Morehead City. Aycock Brown, who would later gain recognition for his photographs and promotion of the Outer Banks, was a civilian investigator for the navy charged with identifying bodies. He sought out Lt. Cunningham for Union Jacks with which to bury four British seamen who had washed ashore near Nags Head. Lt. Cunningham gave him six flags.

Late at night on May 11, 1942, the German submarine U-558 hit the *Bedfordshire* from 600 meters. On May 14 Coast Guardsman Arnold Tolson of Hatteras was patrolling Ocracoke beach when he spotted a body in the surf. Returning with the body to the village he was told of

Photo Credit: Ann Ehringhaus

another victim, which he also retrieved. Aycock Brown was called from Morehead to investigate and immediately recognized the body of Lt. Cunningham. Wahab Howard also identified him by a distinct ring he recalled from their evening together. The other body was identified by

Every year on May 11, a memorial service is held at the British Cemetery to honor the British seamen.

papers on his person as Stanley Craig, Ordinary Telegraphist of the Royal Navy.

The men were buried in boxes procured by the Coast Guard, on land donated by the

Photo Courtesy: Ocracoke Preservation Society

The British sailors buried here were crewmen aboard the the HMS Bedfordshire, *shown above, a British trawler equipped for anti-submarine duty.*

Directions:

Next to the British Cemetery.

Williams family, draped in the two extra Union Jacks given to Brown by Lt. Cunningham, with a full complement of pall bearers. Mr. Amasa Fulcher (Site #7) conducted the service and sang a solo hymn. A week later a Coast Guard patrol boat pulled two more bodies from the water. Unidentifiable due to decomposition, but clad in the same dark blue turtlenecks as Craig and Cunningham, the decision was made to bury these men alongside them. Islanders once more donated their goods and time to honor the sailors.

10. Howard-Wahab-Williams Family Cemeteries

Typical of the approximately 80 family plots on the island, these cemeteries are built on high ground to prevent caskets from floating away in hurricane floodwater. One of the largest and oldest family plots on Ocracoke, this graveyard contains several astonishing markers. You can search for the boy who died before he was born and see the final resting place of Ann Howard, who died on November 24, 1841, at the age of

117. Stories passed down through the family say that in her final year she was bedridden but her mind was still sharp. According to another source, "She did not die of old age; she died of a broken hip." Her epitaph reads "Lo! the prisoner is released/ Lightened of her fleshly load/ Where the weary are at rest/ She is gathered unto God."

The Howard-Wahab-Williams Family Cemetery.

11. Millard Filmore Williams, Jr. House

458 Back Road

Millard Filmore Williams, Jr. had this home built in the early 1900s across the street from his parents' home. Williams and his brother captained schooners carrying freight between Ocracoke and Washington, NC. Before Cockle Creek was dredged, cargo and passengers had to be transferred to lay boats in order to enter the shallow harbor. The lay boats were shallow-draft skiffs that laid out back of the reef while waiting for the larger vessels. The reef is the shallow bar extending the length of the sound side. The first car reached Ocracoke atop two lay boats planked together.

In 1927 the house was raised from 1-1/2 to 2 stories. The porch is more adorned than similar island homes, with diagonal tongue-and-groove sheathing, heavy turned posts and spindled railings. It now belongs to the Fletcher family.

Directions:
Return to the Amasa Fulcher House and head left onto the back road. Walk about two blocks. The next site is 458 Back Road and is on the left.

Directions:

Proceed up the Back Road. Site 12 is just by the Island Girl on the right.

Edgar Howard, banjo, and Maurice Ballance on guitar in 1980.

Photo Credit: Ann Ehringhaus

12. Elmo Cleveland Gaskins House

Built in the 1930s, this was one of the Paddy's Holler houses. For years men "had to go in the woods" to drink and play cards, but it was accepted in this cluster of homes, which also included the Tom Frank Gaskins house (Site #13). Located on a high wooded spot on the outskirts of the village, this home was the location of much music-, merry- and meal-wine making, frowned upon by some. Walter Howard spent his share of time there and wrote a song in the late 1940s with these lyrics:

Wid was on a spree he had fiddled all night free
And they had to hold him up by the collar.
But like a knight of old he grew mighty bold
and hollered out 'Hooray for Paddy's Holler.'

Now in the olden days no one offered praise
For anybody's living at the Holler.
And the town is in a lurch 'cause when they go to church
They all have to pass through Paddy's Holler.

The Howards the O'Neals the Burrus' the Peeles
Well they've all found their way to Paddy's Holler.
It's the choicest spot in town nobody seems to frown
When someone hollers 'Let's go up the Holler!'

Featured Shopping:
• Island Girl .... page 92

Debbie Wells, a watercolor artist who recently attached a small studio to the house, is the proud owner of this colorful home.

13. Tom Frank Gaskins House

This home was built around 1883. A traditional story-and-a-jump house, it is one of a handful not enlarged. Typical features of this style home include a steep gable roof, end chimney, front porch, rear kitchen ell, cedar shaking, habitable attic and tongue-and-groove interior walls. The front door opens to a main family room, with an enclosed stair along the partition wall. The chimney would have been for a coal-burning stove, as wood was scarce.

All of Tom Frank's children were born in the house, but it was his son Joe (1887-1967) for whom the house is known. After Joe's wife's death he claimed she "came in through the keyhole" to check on him. After his death no one was eager to care for his old dog, so the dog was shot and buried with him, although "maybe not in the actual casket."

Photo Courtesy: Bertha O'Neal

Directions:

Backtrack one house and look for the oyster shell path on the left. You'll see a wooden sign shaped like a goose directing you down Fig Tree Lane. This path is for walking and cycling only. It passes close to several homes. Please don't disturb the residents' privacy.

The second house on the left is Site 13.

The gentleman to the left is Tom Frank Gaskins around 1900.

Howard Street

A remaining unpaved bastion of old Ocracoke, Howard Street is not only one of the loveliest streets on the island, but also the most fabled. Howard is the oldest documented family name on the island, and many in the family claim, with varying degrees of pride, that they are direct descendents of Blackbeard's quartermaster, William Howard.

In 1759 a William Howard purchased Ocracoke for 105 pounds. This means Howard would have been a very young man in 1718 when Blackbeard was killed and beheaded. After the battle in Ocracoke waters, the surviving members of his 14-man crew were tried in Virginia. Most were executed, though a William Howard was pardoned by Virginia's royal governor. As quartermaster, Howard would have had knowledge of the location of hidden treasures, perhaps enabling him to buy his life. Ocracoke, and the Outer Banks as a whole, attracted people who wished to live on the margins of society. The assertion that modern Ocracoke Howards descend from a pirate is not incredible.

What is known with certainty is that William Howard, the first resident owner of Ocracoke, sold half the island to his friend John Williams shortly after he purchased it. The two men continued to parcel and sell land and the village grew. Most of the lots along Howard Street still belong to descendents of the original settlers. 𝒞

Photo Credit: Ann Ehringhaus

Until 1977 Ocracoke's water system was completely rainwater dependant. Old cisterns like this one at Site 14 were used to catch and hold the water.

VILLAGE STREET, OCRACOKE ISLAND, N. C.

Howard Street as shown in an old postcard.

Directions:

Continue along the footpath and take a left on to Howard Street. The second house on the left is Site 14.

14. Simon and Sarah Garrish House

This story-and-a-jump home has undergone renovations since its 1888 construction. The front gabled dormers add light and space to the upstairs, and a rear addition replaced the original detached kitchen. The first residents were Simon Garrish Jr. (1865-1935) and his wife Sarah "Miss Sade" Howard Garrish (1870-1961). Tall trees were not abundant on

Photo credit: Standard Oil of New Jersey Collection, University of Louisville

"Miss Sade" reading in her living room in 1955.

Ocracoke, so Simon and Tom W. Howard salvaged timbers from the wreck of the "Old Bateman" and brought them to the site by horse and cart. Tradition says the brickwork used in the chimney was ballast from a cargo ship.

The most recent inhabitant was Elsie Ballance Garrish, who served the island as a nurse when there was no formal medical center. Her husband, Irvin Garrish, was the island's first county commissioner and Simon and Miss Sade's grandson.

Directions:

Proceed up Howard Street to the first house with a picket fence on the right.

15. Hatton and Chloan Howard House

Built around 1904 for Washington Bradford Howard, who soon moved to Newport News, VA, this home was the residence of Hatton Hoover Howard (1880-1942) and Chloan O'Neal Howard (1882-1932). Though the single story with steep hip roof and shed porch design is familiar throughout mainland North Carolina, it is unusual for Ocracoke. The cistern in the yard would have supplied the family with fresh water. The Howard's son, Taft, and wife, Elizabeth Gaskins, lived in the home, which is now the residence of their son and his wife.

16. Gaskins-O'Neal House

An 1883 deed transfers this property from Solomon Howard to William (Bill) W. Gaskins (1841-1916). It mentions buildings on the property, though these were apparently torn down around the time this home was built. Bill Gaskins' parents lived in the little yellow house across the street, which is believed to be the oldest on the island. He was the carpenter who built the Lawrence and Stacy Howard homes (Site #18). The gabled front windows are likely later additions to the story-and-a-jump design. Bill married Dorcas Spencer (b. 1858), and they sold the property to Stanley and Mozelle O'Neal.

Stanley was the last Ocracoker to live in the house. Though hard of hearing he didn't wear a hearing aid. His nephew tells a story of a 1950s visitor who was document-ing the use of cisterns and wanted to film Stanley walking from the house to draw a dipper of water to drink. Stanley, due to his deafness, didn't understand the purpose of the exercise, and may not have understood what an 8 mm camera was. The filmmaker kept sending Stanley back into the house, and each successive take shows him emerg-

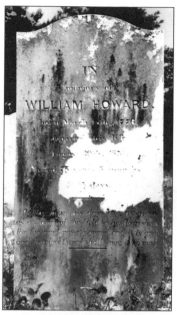

William Howard's gravemarker showing that he lived between 1776 and 1851 can be seen at Site 10.

Directions:

Across the street just to the right of the green house with the Dicies sign.

Photo Courtesy: Lucy Dearing

Stanley O'Neal (left), nephew Philip Howard and Marvin Howard on the porch in the late 1940s. Marvin Howard was the scoutmaster of the pony riding Boy Scouts.

Directions:

Site 17 is on the opposite side of the street. Look for the white house with red trim facing away from Howard Street.

ing with an increasingly bewildered look. He must have wondered at the strange ways of off-islanders.

17. Capt George Gregory Howard House

This turn-of-the-century home faces away from Howard Street toward the harbor. George Gregory Howard (1841-1916) was a schooner captain who spent most of his time at sea while his wife, Mary Francis Gaskill (1846-1920), and family lived in Washington, NC. A few years before his retirement he had this house built, and they returned to live on Ocracoke. Both Captain George and Mary Francis are buried in a family plot across from the Village Craftsman.

Son William Hinman Howard inherited the home but died in 1918, just two years after his father and two years before his mother. His wife, Merian "Miss Mame" Spencer Howard, lived until 1963. Their niece Ruth was married to Sam Jones (see sidebar), and the home was Jones' first island retreat. It was at this time that the distinctive cupola was added. Ruth's brother Carleton Kelly lived in the house for many years, and it now is the residence of Ruth and Sam's daughter.

Photo Courtesy: Susie Scott O'Neal

18. Lawrence Howard House and Stacy Howard House

These similar side-by-side homes were the residences of brothers Lawrence and Stacy Wilson Howard, sons of Perry Coleman Howard (1835-1902) and Ann Mariah Williams (1850-1930), whose graves are near the homes. Their fraternal grandparents were Solomon and Love Tolson Howard, who were the parents of Captain George Gregory Howard (Site #17).

A few years after Perry's death his widow had their old house torn down and a new, two-story house built on the site. However, she continued to use the detached kitchen from her first home. Her son Stacy had the second home built. Bill Gaskins, who lived just down the road in the Gaskins-O'Neal house (Site #16), was in his 60s when he built the houses between 1906 and 1912. Both houses were originally two-story, three-bay-wide homes. The kitchens, dining rooms and pantries that form an ell at the rear

A photo of the Howard House from the early 1930s before the addition of the dormer windows and cupola. This photo was taken from the front of the house.

Directions:
As you continue down the lane look for the Howard Street sign. These houses are just to the left.

Featured Shopping:
• Village Craftsmen ...... page 96

Photo Credit: Ann Ehringhaus

The Stacy Howard House taken in the early 1990s.

Directions:

At the end of Howard Street look to your left and you'll see Site 19.

of the houses were added later. Still later additions provided the luxury of indoor bathrooms. Both homes appear much as they would have after completion.

Blanche Howard Jolliff, the daughter of Stacy and Elizabeth Ballance Howard, resides in the one on the right that belonged to her parents. A font of wisdom about Howard Street and the Howard clan in general, she can sometimes be spotted on her roof cleaning the gutters that lead to her cistern.

19. Ocracoke School

Ocracoke's public K-12 school was constructed in 1973 after the demolition of the 1917 school building that stood on the same site. The first graduating class in 1938 had three students. Prior to that families who could afford to do so sent their children to high school at Washington Collegiate Institute in Washington, NC.

In the elementary grades it was typical, because of the small class size, for teachers to alternate instruction between several grades in the same classroom. This continues to be true. The old school's library was central to the floor plan, and it contained a potbellied stove around which students could gather to work on lessons, read or chat. On particularly cold and rainy days classes would continue until 1 p.m. and then students were released for the day. The school still has no cafeteria, and the majority of

Photo Courtesy: Betty Helen Chamberlin

students walk or bike home for lunch, though inclement weather would no longer be an excuse to not return. In late spring, however, modern high schoolers sometimes find themselves unable to pass up particularly nice afternoons on the beach.

The Ocracoke School built in 1917 was used until 1971 when it was replaced by the current building on this site.

Isabel Morris, a 1941 graduate, remembers that in the late 1930s one of the teachers was a gifted pianist. During the lunch break she would often play and students would sing and dance. Each spring, in preparation for the graduation ceremony, high schoolers would go to Springer's Point to gather ivy and flowers to decorate the stage. Each grade participated in

Photo credit: Standard Oil of New Jersey Collection , University of Louisville

the commencement exercises. Ocracoke School continues to graduate between one and 14 students each year.

Directions:

From the end of Howard Street take a right and look for Deepwater Pottery and Books To Be Red on your left. This is site 20.

20. Frederick and Dezzie Bragg House

Artists and a romantic tale have attached themselves to this turn-of-the-19th-century home. In the 1960s it was the residence of artist JoKo. Today it is the site of the Ocrafolk festival each June.

Photo Credit: Ann Ehringhaus

Island musicians and story tellers of all ages delight summer visitors at the Ocrafolk Opry.

Buried to the left of the porch is a woman named Sally who was called "Aunt Soot." Local tradition holds that Aunt Soot was a free black, perhaps from the West Indies, who met an early, otherwise unidentified Bragg while working in the village as a domestic. The two fell in love and applied for a marriage license that was denied because Bragg didn't have any black blood. Not to be so easily confounded, the lovers cut themselves, shared blood and were married. (In 1829 a Thomas Bragg of Carteret County— of which Ocracoke was then a part—married a woman whose name was not given.) In his book, *The Waterman's Song: Slavery and Freedom in Maritime North Carolina,* David S. Cecelski observes that race relations were not as restrictive on the Outer Banks as in the plantation south. However, Aunt Soot and Bragg's marriage would certainly have been an exceptional event.

Thomas Bragg purchased this property in the 1820s. He had a house on this site that his grandson Frederick razed in order to build this home. Notice the steep pyramidal roof. In 1916 Frederick delivered a load of lumber for the construction of the school, and his wife, Miss Dezzie, is remembered for always keeping a dipper by her cistern for thirsty school children.

21. Capt. Thurston and Nora Gaskill House

Originally set on a large tract of land, this 1925 home is now surrounded by homes belonging to the children, grandchildren and great-grandchildren of the first owners, Thurston and Helen Gaskill. Capt. "Tony" Thurston worked for 72 years as perhaps the most popular, knowledgeable and skilled hunting guide on the island. As a boy he participated in commercial hunts before the 1917 Migratory Bird Act made the large-scale killing of waterfowl illegal. He mentored a number of islanders who work on the water, and his family members carry on the traditions of hunting and fishing.

Capt. Thurston had a special method of boat maintenance. A man who was an adolescent in the 1950s recalls with a smile, "Thurston Gaskill used to say, 'I'm gonna take you fishing today.' He'd take us boys out there, drop a line over. 'Ah, they ain't biting today. Jump overboard, scrub the bottom of my boat.' And we'd scrub her off and he'd bring us back."

Today his granddaughter Marlene Matthews runs a bed and breakfast in the home.

Featured Accommodation:
• Thurston House B&B
.... page 112

Directions:
Take a left at the stop sign. You'll see site 21 just 20 yards up the street on the left.

Photo Courtesy: Marlene Mathews

Captain "Tony" Thurston Gaskill at his hunting camp.

Mail Boats & the Post Office

Modern visitors to Ocracoke may feel removed from the rest of the world. But before private ferry operations began between Ocracoke and Hatteras in the 1950s, services and transport were even more infrequent. The majority of islanders and visitors, traveling without the luxury of private plane or boat, arrived and departed on the mail boat. Each year, local captains bid on the right to make the daily round trip, save on Sunday, to Atlantic to haul Ocracoke's mail. These vessels also ferried passengers, who shared space with the mail, freight and groceries. Most people preferred to sit on deck and avoid the close confines of the cabin, for reasons many stories make abundantly clear. A crowded summertime boat would have carried 35 people who vied amicably for prime seats on

Photo credit: Standard Oil of New Jersey Collection, University of Louisville

Local men unloading the mail boat in the 1950s.

the afterdeck under a canvas awning. Gallant men and adventurous boys ended up on the cabin top or on boxes of fish or freight. The three-and-a-half-hour journey was a time for sharing picnic baskets and stories. Tourists were likely to disembark with newfound friends.

For off-islanders, traveling on the mail boat was a novelty. The cramped yet cozy journeys are vividly recalled, as often for poor weather and queasy stomachs as for the camaraderie inspired by a passage across the sound. Captain Elmo Fulcher ran the mailboat *Aleta* for more than 20 years. His brother-in-law, Nathaniel Jackson, a native Ocracoker, remembers crossing the sound in a thick fog. Capt. Elmo knew the route so well that even without visibility or sophisticated navigational instruments he could accurately predict when the boat would

scrape the next buoy. The mailboat *Dolphin* was piloted by Captain Ansley O'Neal. In one story, a young boy traveling to visit family was in the pilothouse when Capt. Ansley, needing both hands to tend to a task, deliberately stabbed his pocket knife into his leg, only to casually retrieve it shortly thereafter. The awed boy would later learn that Capt. Ansley had a wooden leg.

Sidenotes

Photo Courtesy: Larry Williams

The first air mail from Ocracoke to Kitty Hawk, October 12, 1937.

Sidenotes 🌿

Photo Card Courtesy: Betty Helen Chamberlin

Big Ikes Store and Post Office.

Rough seas and playful captains set the stage for the boat's arrival in port. By all accounts, this was *the* event of the day throughout the 1940s and '50s. The mail boat's arrival in mid-afternoon served to connect Ocracoke to the rest of the world, bringing friends, news and necessities. Philip Howard, a current resident who traces his ancestry to early settlers, spent childhood summers amidst his island clan. He recalls, "Everybody would be waiting on the dock. As a kid, it seemed like the only time anything exciting would happen. You'd see who was on the boat. Everybody would greet each other." People would help unload the cargo, and postmistress Elizabeth Howard sorted the mail, which was distributed by calling out people's names (a neighbor or friend would deliver it if someone happened to be absent), leading to the unique island phrase "call the mail over."

Photo Card Courtesy: Betty Helen Chamberlin

Old Post Office, with Thomas Wallace Howard, postmaster.

The island's first post office was built close to where the mail boat docked. Now a rental cottage, it still contains the original boxes. Ocracoke outgrew the brick post office that replaced the first one, and in 2000 the post office was moved to its current location on the edge of town.

Ocracokers still rely heavily on the post office to communi-cate with one another. On a recent December day, the post office bulletin board held the addresses

Mail truck on the ferry.

Photo Card Courtesy: Ocracoke Preservation Society

of a young man serving overseas and an older man recovering from a hospital visit; an invitation to a baby shower; a reminder of where and when to meet for caroling; the ubiquitous "housing wanted" and "lost bike" announcements; a list of building permit applications; a letter of thanks to those who made cookies for Meals on Wheels; an open-ended inquiry, "Do you skateboard and think it's time for a half-pipe?"; and newspaper clippings with on-going commentary and rebuttals scrawled in the margins. At the post office you always run into friendly and familiar faces, and more often than not there's a tidbit of gossip to pick up. The habits of the past continue to define the present. ✔

Directions:
Turn around and head back down Highway 12. Look for Oscar's House on your left.

Featured Accommodation:
• Oscar's House B&B . page 110

Featured Recreation:
• Therapeutic Massage..page 81

Featured Shopping:
• Ocracoke Restoration page 81

Photo Courtesy: Ocracoke Preservation Society

Captain Joe Burrus at work atop the Ocracoke Light.

Directions:
Continue on Highway 12 and make a left on Lighthouse Road. Site 23 is on your left.

Featured Accommodation:
• The Island Inn .... page 111

22. Capt. Joseph Burrus House

The building now called Oscar's House was built in 1940 as the retirement home of Capt. Joseph Burrus, who between 1929 and 1946 served as the lightkeeper on Ocracoke. Capt. Joe was a native of Hatteras who spent 45 years in the U.S. Lighthouse Service. His first wage in 1903 was for $30 a month. His stations were often at lights offshore, living in a spartan structure 40 feet above the water. The keeper was responsible for maintaining and lighting oil lamps in several dozen buoys. After several lonely weeks the keepers would switch, bringing with them the needed fuel, food and supplies. Once Captain Joe was frozen in for almost a month; after he ran out of tobacco he chewed boat caulking. A happier occasion was the time his wife and six children arrived with Christmas dinner, presents and a tree.

After his death the home passed to his son Oscar, who guided fishing and hunting trips. In 1982 Ann Ehringhaus, a photographer and the author of *Ocracoke Portrait*, purchased the home from Capt. Joe's granddaughter. Since 1984 she has operated it as a bed and breakfast and retreat center.

23. Island Inn/Odd Fellows Lodge

The central two-storied part of this inn was completed in 1901 and served as the island's first public school and the local Oddfellows Lodge. In 1920 Benjamin O'Neal purchased the building to use as a private residence and hired Charlie Scarborough to move it across the street to its current location. According to Mr. Charlie's grandson, a large number of men showed up to assist, one of whom was known to be a lay-about and grumbler. Charlie indicated a stump and said that man was to sit there, complain

This photo, taken at the turn of the last century, shows students at the first public school on the island.

about the heat, the mosquitoes, the strenuous work, the low pay and the mismanagement. For his griping he would receive the same 35 cents as the other workers, who were to recognize his expertise in this matter and leave the moaning to him. This tactic, Mr. Charlie theorized, guaranteed everyone a shorter workday.

Around 1940 Stanley Wahab (Site #6) purchased the building for $700. He converted the

After use as a school, a men's social club and a dance hall, this building became the Silver Lake Inn. Today it is the Island Inn.

downstairs into a coffee shop and the upstairs to a rooming house, later a naval officer's club. The addition of several former Navy barracks created a dance hall, and in the 1950s the two-story east wing was built for a dining hall and

Directions:

Continue down Lighthouse Road and look for a small green sign on your left , "The Boathouse."

White Friends Hold Last Rites For Negro Man

OCRACOKE — Leonard Bryant, 82, a member of the only Negro family on Ocracoke, died last week.

Funeral services were conducted Nov. 16 in the Methodist Church, of which he had been a member and sexton for many years. Since there is no segregation in the church, he had taken communion with the white members during that time. All pallbearers at the funeral were white.

He was buried in the unsegregated community cemetery.

Bryant came to Ocracoke at the age of 19 to help the late George Credle run the old Ponder Hotel. He lived alone in a home adjacent to that of other members of his family; his wife, who has been ill, has been living with a daughter in Winston-Salem.

Survivors include a son, Julius, and two daughters, Mildred and Muse Pryant, all of Ocracoke, and other children, in addition to his wife.

The obituary from the 1960s.

guest rooms. This local landmark continues to welcome visitors and serve up island fare.

24. Mildred and Musel Bryant House

This home was built before 1910, perhaps in the last quarter of the 1800s, and belonged to the only black family to settle on Ocracoke after the Civil War. Leonard Bryant came to Ocracoke at age 19 to help run the Grand Ponder Hotel (Site #2). His daughter Mildred Bryant bought this house in 1949 and lived in its three rooms with her sister, Muse, for more than 40 years. (At this writing Miss Musie, born in 1904, is the oldest living islander.) In *Ocracokers* Mildred explains the building's original use as part of the Lifesaving Station: "It used to set about a hundred yards down the road toward the lighthouse. This was the boathouse for the boats that they used in the ocean. The beach used to come up almost to my backyard then. They kept two boats on carts, and they had these big government horses to drag the things down to the beach."

The front and rear double door openings have since been filled in, the house has been raised and a workshop added underneath. The home retains cedar shingling and brushy landscaping to protect it from wind and serves as a reminder of islanders' continued willingness to salvage and adapt.

25. Selma and Benjamin E. Spencer House

180 Lighthouse Road

Directions:
You'll find the next site about 30 yards up the road on your right. (The third house on your right.)

Thad Gaskins built this home for Benjamin Early and Selma Wise Spencer in 1937, three years after their marriage. Some of the wood for its construction came from the schooner *Nomis*, which in 1935 wrecked offshore with a cargo of 338,000 feet of lumber. When their home was first built the couple had a harbor view from the back windows, and when the sea was rough the breakers were visible from their front porch.

Miss Selma, born in 1905 near Arapahoe, NC, came to Ocracoke to teach and served as the school principal between 1946 and 1948. A former student says she commanded respect without inspiring fear. She was also a devoted Sunday School teacher at the Methodist Church. Ben worked on dredge boats and met Selma while home on leave. During the early years of their marriage he worked mulletting, shrimping, oystering, laying brick, hauling sand and building. By the 1960s he was a popular and busy charter boat captain. Benjamin Early died in 1975. His bride outlived him by 20 years, and the house is often called "Miss Selma's house."

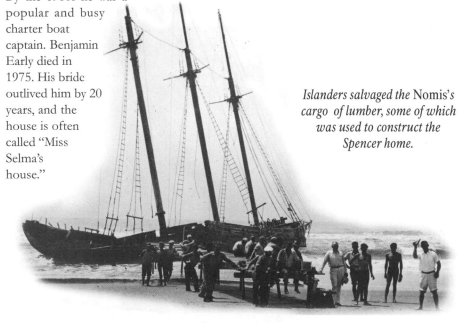

Islanders salvaged the Nomis's *cargo of lumber, some of which was used to construct the Spencer home.*

Photo Courtesy: Ocracoke Preservation Society

Directions:
Proceed to the next house on the right. The O'Neal house is located at the back of the lot.

26. Eliza and William I. O'Neal House

196 Lighthouse Road

Before Silver Lake was dredged in the 1930s and 1940s two small creeks divided the island. They ran where Highway 12 now passes between the Island Inn (Site #24) and Spencer's Market. People living to the southwest near the lighthouse are known as Pointers, while those living on the northeast side of the harbor are called Creekers. The distinction was both geographic and civic. The disparate groups maintained their own churches, stores and to some extent, social circles. Today you might hear a local joke about "getting back down point where I belong," or roll her eyes and quip "you know how those Creekers are."

This home was built in 1910 for William and Eliza O'Neal near Northern Pond, close to where William had grown up. His bride was unhappy living with few other families around, so in 1928 the home was dismantled and moved down point to its present location. During the reconstruction, William, his brother and two other men went fishing. They had left under starry skies but returned in lashing rain and low visibility. Their

Photo Credit: Ann Ehringhaus

The O'Neal House.

This photo shows one of two bridges spanning "the Gut" or creek that divided the island. This photo was taken in the late 1930s before the Navy filled in the creek.

Post Card Courtesy: Michael G. Tames

boat capsized just outside the entrance to the harbor. The men were wearing hip boots. Three of them, including William, were unable to free themselves from the tangle of nets trapped under the boat. Eliza took a job at the Pamlico Inn (Site #29) and raised their four young children alone.

Their daughter Isabella Morris, who worked as a schoolteacher in Carteret County for 27 years, now lives in the home.

Another view of "the Gut" bridge.

27. Nathan Spencer House

255 Lighthouse Road

As on Howard Street, the bulk of houses on Lighthouse Road are historic and inhabited by islanders. The wrap-around porch and pyramidal roof on this home distinguish it from the two other foursquare houses on the street. Built sometime before 1922, it was the home of Nathan (1882-1947) and Louisa Simpson Spencer (1884-

Directions:

Continue on Lighthouse Road. Site 27 is on the left several houses down. Look for house number 255.

Photo Courtesy: Family of Lawton Howard

1966). His brother Sommers and her sister Esther were also married and lived next door. Nathan and Louisa lost one son in infancy and raised three others—Herman, Sommers and Murray. The family grave plot is visible from the street.

Sommers (1911-1979) and his wife, Etta Carter Styron, inherited the property. Miss Etta continues to reside in the home, in daily contact with her grandchildren and great-grandchildren.

Directions:

Just up the street to the right.

An 1898 photo shows the lighthouse and keeper's quarters taken when the lighthouse was just 75 years old.

28. Lighthouse and Keeper's Quarters

After a 1798 beacon on Shell Castle Island in the inlet failed due to shifting sands, a local family deeded land to the government for construction of a lighthouse. Noah Porter, a mason from Massachusetts, built the Ocracoke Lighthouse for a cost to U.S. taxpayers of $11,359.35. Completed in 1823, it is the oldest structure on the island, the oldest operating light in North Carolina and the second oldest on the East Coast. The only time

Bamber Photo Courtesy: Ocracoke Preservation Society

169. C. S. 1. OCRACOKE LIGHT STATION, N. C. MAY 24,1898.

the lighthouse wasn't in use was during WWII when it would have silhouetted ships at sea, making them visible targets for submarines. Approximately 70 feet tall, constructed of brick and heavily whitewashed, the 8,000 candlepower light is visible 14 miles at sea.

Porter also built an adjacent one-story, three-room brick house as keeper's quarters, which was expanded in 1897 to two stories and refurbished in 1950 to include indoor plumbing. The first keeper was responsible for the oil lamp and reflecting glass, which was replaced by a Fresnel lens in 1854. During the years before electric light it must have been a dramatic sight and a comfort to mariners and their families. Captain Joe Burrus (Site #22) was the last keeper. Listed on the National Register of Historic Places, today it is maintained by the National Park Service.

29. Site of Pamlico Inn

Islanders born before 1930 often say there was more entertainment in their day than now. A turn-of-the-century hotel stood at the end of this road. In 1913 Captain Bill Gaskill, the father of Thurston Gaskill (Site #21), purchased the business and renamed it the Pamlico Inn. Tourists used the inn as a staging point for hunting and fishing and also as a retreat. Locals fondly remember the large dance floor at the water's edge as the site of many good times. In the 1930s the competing Wahab Village Hotel (now Blackbeard's Lodge) also had a dance floor, as well as a movie theater and roller-skating rink. At that time the school often showed silent movies, and islanders habitually gathered on private porches to play

Directions:
Straight down Lighthouse Road the horizon is visible over the road. This is the soundfront location of Site 29. The Pamlico Inn once stood here.

JAMIE STYRON BATHING PARTY 1917- BEST LOOKING GAL IS ANNIE SPRINGER

A 1917 bathing party from the old hotel that became the Pamlico Inn. The Inn can be seen in the background.

Photo Courtesy: Larry will ams

Image Courtesy: Marlene Mathews

Pamlico Inn On Ocracoke Island, Established by Late Captain Bill Gaskill, and Operated Today By David Gaskill Is Still A Most Popular Place For Sportsmen And Vacationists To Stop

OCRACOKE'S PAMLICO INN is pictured above with its operator David Gaskill anding beneath the sign. This famous hostelry which has included among its guests, ortsmen and vacationists from all parts of the world was established by the late Capt. ill Gaskill. It was at Pamlico Inn that the N. C. Young Republican's on an Invitation leeting and Convention at Ocracoke made their headquarters. Pamlico Inn also caters a number of families who take their children there because they like its location which directly on the Sound-side of the island.—Photo and cut courtesy Elizabeth City Ad-ance).

instruments, sing and dance. Fiddles, pianos and guitars were especially popular.

The Pamlico Inn is also remembered for large fuel tanks that sat near the water's edge next to the hotel. One winter in the early 1930s one of the tanks was left slightly open or developed a leak. Something sparked and a giant explosion ensued. It was the middle of the night and it "rocked the whole island," says Blanche Styron, who was 8 or 9 at the time. She recalls that it was a cold night with a bright moon shining. People on the creek side of the island rushed toward the flames to see what was going on. Meanwhile, people living down point were hurrying in the other direction because, as one man says, "they thought their time had come." Most of the island's populace ended up gathered outside to witness the fire and piece events together.

There must have been no breeze that night

because only the fuel tanks burned. The Pamlico Inn remained a thriving business and social center until it was damaged beyond repair by the 1944 hurricane.

30. Albert Styron Store and Albert Styron House

In 1920 Albert "Big Albert" Styron floated wood from his home on Hog Island to build this general store. An adventurous and active man, Big Albert soon tired of shopkeeping, so his wife Mamie Spencer and their children ran the store. Islanders could buy molasses, fuel, fish, meal, chicken feed, bed ticking or meats and eggs raised by the family.

The neighboring Colonial Revival foursquare house was either built about the same time or enlarged from an existing home. Daughter Mary Anderson is the current owner and resident. The Styrons' had one of the first televisions on the island. A local man recalls the early days of TV on Ocracoke, "I can remember everyone gathering around to watch the Friday night fights. This little bitty screen, black and white. You'd hear somebody say 'pretty good reception tonight' and there'd be a black guy and a white guy [fighting]. You couldn't tell which was which."

Having spent his life gill netting, pound netting, mulleting, shrimping and floundering, Big Albert found it impossible to leave the water for

Directions:
Walk back down Lighthouse Rd and you'll see the store on your left. Then take a left on to Creek Road. The Albert Styron House is number 106.

The Albert Styron Store in 1980.

long. After a heart attack, in spite of doctor's orders, he continued going out in his boat. In March 1956 he left to seed oyster beds and never returned. His 18-foot motor boat was discovered with his wallet, social security card and wrist watch inside, though his body was never recovered.

The store closed in 1975 after the death of Mamie and Big Albert's youngest son, Albert Jr. It was restored and re-opened between 1991 and 2004 by Candy Gaskill, a great granddaughter . Her sister, Vlaerie Mason, currently runs Village Print from the storefront. (Valerie desinged many of the ads in the guidebook section.)

Directions:

Go to the last house on the right facing Creek Road.

Shown below is a portion of the 1915 panorama taken from the lighthouse.

31. Leon Austin House

Capt. Wesley Austin from Hatteras was appointed Keeper of the Ocracoke Light in 1912 and purchased this property from John McWilliams (Site #32). In the early 1920s he deeded a portion of land to his son Leon Austin and daughter-in-law Mary Frances O'Neal. Before the 1937 dredging of Cockle Creek, marsh grass spread from the water's edge, and Leon and Mary Frances' 1925 four-room story-and-a-jump house with a hip-roofed front porch was constructed on a small rise on the property. They had two daughters, Ruby and Louise, the younger of whom was born in the house.

When he retired from the Lighthouse Service, Captain Wesley constructed the adjacent home that is now the Lightkeeper's Inn. His grand-daughters would have been frequent visitors, as the families shared a cistern.

The Austin family sold the home in 1973, and it passed through many owners, serving briefly as a doctor's residence and the island's medical center. Over the years the front porch was enclosed and asbestos shingles added. In the mid-1990s the house was restored to more closely resemble its original condition. The front dormer addition is a modern renovation.

32. John Wilson McWilliams House

One of the more ornamented island homes, this late Victorian was built around 1880 for John Wilson McWilliams. Unlike most island lots, this one was never subdivided, and the home retains a large lawn. The family owned cattle and sheep, which grazed on what is now Park Service land, and sold the wool to off-island markets. In the 1920s and '30s the McWilliams family had a department store, fish house and net house on docks at the front of the property. The department store, which sold furniture and household goods, went out of

Directions:
Walk towards the harbor on Creek Road. Take a left on to Silver Lake Drive. Site 32 is on the left set back from the road.

Photo Courtesy: Ocracoke Preservation Society

Photo by Ann Ehringhaus

*The McWilliams House is on
the right in this photo from
the 1980s.*

Directions:

Facing the McWilliams House,
look to your right and locate the
two-story house with blue
shutters.

business during the Depression. The fish house supplied the Fulton Fish Market in New York. All of the buildings were lost in the 1944 hurricane.

McWilliams moved to Black Mountain, NC, around 1910, hoping to relieve his tuberculosis, and left the home to Charlie Caswell "Charlie Mac" and Hilda Tolson McWilliams. The house was sold out of the family in 1986 to Keith and Isabel McDermott, who received the Ocracoke Preservation Society award for their efforts to rehabilitate the structure. They use it as a vacation home.

33. William Charles Thomas House

William Charles Thomas (1857-1930) was a ship captain from Ocracoke whose work took him frequently to the West Indies, and he styled his 1899 home after Caribbean houses he admired. The pierced, sawtoothed bargeboards that ornament all three gables are believed to be original. Two stories of porches complementing the front of the home were destroyed by the hurricane of 1944. The structure remaining square on its foundation may be due to it having one of the early trap floor doors. These doors allow rising water to enter the home. The innovative design is often credited to builder Charlie Scarborough, who no doubt took a lesson

Photo Courtesy: Ocracoke Preservation Society

The Berkley Castle.

from the damaging tidal waters of the 1899 hurricane. People who didn't have them often scuttled their own floors during storm surges.

Long owned by Capt. Thomas' daughter, Lillian Simpson, the house is now a summer residence belonging to Susan Barksdale.

34. Berkley Castle

155 Silver Lake Drive

All Ocracokers over a certain age have stories about Sam Jones (see sidebar), the Norfolk industrialist who hired local carpenters, decoy carvers and boat builders to construct the Berkley Castle in the early 1950s. Driven by a unique vision and fueled by deep pockets, Jones would occasionally insist part of the construction be torn down and rebuilt to accommodate his fancy. The asymmetrical angle on the right wing was part of

Directions:

Turn around and walk towards The Castle.

Featured Accommodations:
• The Castle BB&B .... page 109

Sam Jones

Neither the 20th-century history nor an architectural overview of Ocracoke would be complete without a nod to Sam Jones. By all accounts an eccentric and often generous man, Jones was born in Swan Quarter on the mainland of Hyde County in 1893. At age 13 he left school, and in his early 20s he started work at the Berkley Machine Works and Foundry Co. in Norfolk, Virginia. Six years later he bought the company, remained true to his work ethic and grew to be a wealthy man. As a boy Jones attended a July 4th pony-penning here, and in 1939 he visited the island with his first wife. His love affair with Ocracoke lasted until his death.

Many credit Jones as being the primary economy on Ocracoke during the 1950s. He entertained clients, friends and employees on the island. Wording on his invitation demonstrates his loyalty to the island and its residents: "Ocracoke remains in its primitive state; it clings to its easy-going solitude. It is different. Ocracokers don't object to some modernization but they aim for their island to retain its unique flavor. They glory in doing things the old, hard way. They are friendly, unhurried, and welcome visitors to the island. The Islanders are the best, and most willing workers I have ever worked with. Let's go!" He hired local men as builders and to guide hunting and fishing trips, and he employed local women as cooks and housekeepers. As one woman who remembers Jones said, "He hired everybody he could."

His first island retreat was the Capt. George Gregory Howard house (Site #17), on Howard

Image Courtesy: Ocracoke Preservation Society

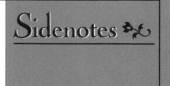

Street, where one of his daughters still lives. After outgrowing that, in the early 1950s he enlarged an old home into the Berkeley Manor (Site #4). Not long after, construction of the Berkley Castle (Site #34) on the other side of the harbor began. On weekends Jones would

Tax Evasion Sentence

Mr Boos:
Just to make sure that you do not miss out on any OF the news.

Manees.

Jones Ready to Enter Prison

By GLENN SCOTT

Virginian-Pilot Staff Writer

NORFOLK — Industrialist Samuel G. Jones Sr. agreed Monday to report to the U.S. marshal here Saturday to begin serving a prison sentence for tax evasion.

Jones, 67, Berkley Machine Works & Foundry Co., Inc., president for 40 years, said he would surrender at 6 a.m. for the 400-mile ride to the federal penitentiary in Lewisburg, Pa.

On March 20 the U.S. Supreme Court refused to hear Jones' appeal. An order for Jones' imprisonment arrived 10 days ago, and U.S. Dist. Judge Walter E. Hoffman said he could no longer stay it.

10-DAY TRIAL

Jones was convicted in U.S. Dist. Court here of evading $277,-000 in income taxes. The May 1959 trial lasted 10 days.

Figuring prominently in the trial were Jones' 600-acre SaJo Farms in Princess Anne County and extensive company holdings

on Ocracoke Island, N.C.

Jones claimed the Ocracoke holdings — Berkley Manor, Samjo Manor and Green Island Gunning Club — were used to entertain prospective customers in lieu of national advertising. He said they were not used for his personal pleasure — an assertion he repeated Monday in a conference with Hoffman.

Hoffman, after the trial, fined Jones $30,000 and imposed five-year sentences, to run concurrently, for each of the six counts.

STUDY TO BE MADE

In sentencing Jones Hoffman used a procedure that will require the Bureau of Prisons to make a study of Jones.

Hoffman said the study was indicated by Jones' "unusual conduct" during the trial and by a preliminary probation report. The study would include Jones' background, abilities, mental and physical health.

During the trial Jones, an outspoken witness, was cited by Hoffman for contempt. Hoffman said

Monday he does not intend to act on the citation.

After three months Hoffman will receive a bureau report which could result in a modification of Jones' sentence.

ADVICE WANTED

"Frankly, Mr. Jones," Hoffman said Monday at the conference requested by Jones, "I don't know what to do with your case." He said he wants advice from bureau experts.

The 90-minute conference also was attended by Jones' attorney, Ellsworth T. Simpson of Washington, and representatives of the U.S. attorney.

Simpson opened the conference by saying Jones wished to present matters of a personal rather than legal nature.

Dr. Edward H. Jones, pastor of First Presbyterian Church, told Hoffman he knew Jones to be a man of "integrity, honor and morality."

Hoffman explained that he knew Jones is a man of standing and good reputation, but he made it

clear that he had no intention of suspending Jones' sentence with probation.

Hoffman stated his belief that Jones does not think he did anything wrong in charging off numerous personal expenses as business costs.

Hoffman said he was "puzzled" because what Jones had done was "obviously wrong."

Jones said again, as he had done throughout his trial, that he had "not taken advantage of anyone."

The industrialist spoke of his philanthropies, his boyhood on a farm, his years of labor. He disputed Hoffman's suggestion that he is a millionaire. He asked for a stay until the death "in a few days" of a cancer-stricken friend.

At the conclusion, Hoffman asked Jones to arrange to surrender to the marshal. Jones said he would report at 6 a.m. Saturday, thus avoiding a night in City Jail. He said he is an early riser.

He shook hands with Hoffman, thanking him for his courtesy in granting the conference.

arrive with a dozen odd guests, usually men here to enjoy his Outer Green Island Gunning and Fishing Club. But on some occasions, the 8,500-square-foot Castle proved too small, and guests spilled over into the Berkley Manor. Great parties would ensue, often with people

Sidenotes

clad in costumes provided by the host. There would be local musicians picking banjos and strumming guitars, guests square dancing and Jones leading the hokey pokey. He loved

Photo Courtesy: Steve & Mary Wright

Sam ensuring that his horse Ikey D enjoys the festivites.

animals and was known to welcome his horse, Ikey D., in to join the fun. Smoking, however, was not allowed inside.

Jones owned several dozen Ocracoke horses and kept them penned at the Berkley Manor. A former member of the Mounted Boy Scout Troop, which was active on the island in the 1950s, recalls: "Sam Jones would sit on his fence and wave a check in the air, and point one [horse] out. Anybody had nerve enough to get up on him, when they got off, he'd give 'em a check." Jones also frequently gave gifts that didn't hinge on bravado. He had a group of women flown to Norfolk to select new dresses for themselves, and on at least one occasion he purchased a truckload of furniture to distribute. He also supported both churches, bought the island's first ambulance and made donations to the boy scouts and fire department.

Unrestrained by social convention, Jones once interrupted a sermon to compliment the preacher on his work.

Jones went on to build a home for his family and a Whittlers' Club for island men. He purchased Springer's Point, a large tract of high land located on the sound west of the lighthouse, which he called "Teach's Castle" or the "old Blackbeard Plantation." Jones once wrote, "the only lasting Monument that we can leave to posterity is what we give of ourselves, of our knowledge and of our experience, which will continue in the lives of others."

At his death in 1977 Jones was buried on Springer's Point next to Ikey D.

Photo Credit: Ann Ehringhaus

Sidenotes

The Whittlers' Club.

his original plan. A 1954 reporter from Manteo wrote, "We visited the impressive architectural efforts of one Sam Jones who had built an imposing structure that dominated the skyline second only to the historic lighthouse. Opinions regarding Sam's house varied among the members of our party, but we all admitted that it was unique and different; a monument to a man who knew what he wanted and made sure he got it."

The finished building was used for lavish entertainment. The oak floors were covered with Oriental rugs, the cypress walls hung with tapestries and oil paintings, the shelves filled with ceramics and the table set with porcelain and crystal. Rain falling on the roof was transported to cisterns in copper gutters.

The Castle stood empty for many years after Jones' 1977 death. In 1994 the building and adjacent properties were purchased for $800,000. Despite financial enticement to sell or raze, owners Steve and Mary Wright renovated, opening The Castle to visitors as a bed and breakfast. Some of the furnishings are original, and the fine craftsmanship of the island builders still impresses.

35. Wagon Wheel Cottages

Only one of these small cottages was built on this site, and the dock was floated from the old post office. Originally part of the Navy base, the buildings were moved to Parkers Creek for use as hunting and fishing camps. After the National Park Service acquired that land in the 1950s, the Gaskill family relocated the buildings, renovating them into cottages. These modest rentals recall the days when visitors valued the island's natural resources above creature comforts. At the time

Featured Accommodations:

• Ocracoke Harbor Inn page 108

Directions:

Continue walking in the same direction until you reach Wagon Wheel Cottages on your right.

The Wagon Wheel Cottages in their original location on the Navy base overlooking the Pamlico Sound.

Photo Courtesy: Betty Helen Chamberlin

they opened, Ocracoke did not have (according to Carl Goerch's 1956 book, *Ocracoke*) policemen or a jail, a traffic light, pool hall, brick building, chain store, hospital, doctor, golf course, parking meter, lawyer, bank, sidewalk, billboard, bowling alley, book store or beer parlor.

Families and sportsmen, loyal to a vision of Ocracoke increasingly disguised by commerce, continually rent the same cottages year after year. The graffiti on the interior walls confirms their appreciation of both the cabins and the island. The wagon wheel from horse-drawn days that once marked the entrance is now gone.

36. Down Point Decoys Gift Shop

Wahab Howard (Site #6) moved this building from the Green Island Hunting Club in the 1950s and turned it into the island's first gift shop, which was opened by Ruth and Bill Cochran around 1960. Their rent was $45 a month. "We just called it the gift shop," says Ruth, who filled the shop with shells and beachcombed treasures. A locally generated newsletter from the time noted, "Ruth has designed a very original ear-bob, using the native sea oats."

For a time the Cochrans ran the Island Inn (Site #23), then called the Hotel Silver Lake, and Bill operated an airlift between Ocracoke and Hatteras. There was not yet an airstrip, so Bill landed the plane on the highway or beach or even next to the Coast Guard station. In 1968 the Cochrans retired to the mainland. Part of Ruth's impressive shell collec-

Directions

Follow Silver Lake Drive until it merges with Hwy. 12. Stay left at the fork and follow the road around the harbor until you see Down Point Decoys on your left.

Featured Recreation
- Ride the Wind .... page 79
- The Slushy Stand .... page 74

Featured Shopping
- Island Ragpicker .... page 91

Photo Courtesy: Larry Williams

A hunter stands in a sink box surrounded by decoys. Sink boxes are unique to Pamlico and Albemarle Sounds and allow hunters to hide in the shallow waters while remaining dry.

Photo Courtesy: Larry Williams

Most of the birds in the picture are decoys, but it's hard to tell the difference, which was the plan.

Directions

Look across the street for the second house in from the corner.

tion is on display at the Ocracoke Preservation Society Museum (Site #1).

The building has been in continual use as a gift shop and remains in the Howard family. It currently houses Down Point Decoys, featuring work by local islander and nationally recognized carver David O'Neal.

37. Jacob and Brittina Williams House

Now confronting the bustle of Highway 12, the houses along the remainder of the tour were built when this section of road was part of Howard Street. This early 1900s home belonged to Jacob (1887-1954) and Brittina "Brittie" (1887-1971) Williams, who were married in 1908. Jacob was the brother of Millard Filmore Williams, Jr. (Site #11). They had five daughters, and Jacob supported the family by fishing. Their daughter Vera and her husband, Lawrence Ballance, raised three children in the home. In their lifetimes they saw the paving of many island roads and neighbor's homes become commercial establishments.

Alton Ballance, a professional educator and the author of *Ocracokers*, lives in the family home. Shady live oaks, cedars, mimosas and yaupon afford a measure of privacy but diminish the breezes his parents and grandparents would have enjoyed while rocking on the front porch during hot summer evenings.

38. Will and Sigma Willis House

285 Highway 12

This 1½-story bungalow with a low hipped roof and an engaged front porch was built sometime between 1924 and 1931. The sills extending the length of the house come from the 1928 shipwreck of the *George W. Truitt*.

Captain Will Willis, who ran one of the mailboats and a general store, bought this property in the 1920s for $750. At that time the land extended to the harbor, where the family built a dock and store (Site #39), and included the lot behind this house as well as a home that had belonged to North Carolinian Josephus Daniels. Daniels served as Secretary of the Navy from 1913 to 1921. FDR served under Daniels and later appointed him Ambassador to Mexico. A photo of the Ocracoke Lighthouse graced the embassy wall during Daniels' tenure. The Daniels' home was destroyed and used for firewood.

The home remains in the Willis family.

If you are standing with Site 37 on your right, the view in this picutre is what you would have seen about 50 years ago.

Directions

Walk past the Pelican Restaurant and look for Village Diva on your right.

Featured Shopping
• Mermaid's Folly .... page 87

A group of friends enjoy a treat at Piland's Ice Cream Parlor, once located near Silver Lake. Seated from the left: Fannie Pearl (McWilliams) Wahab, Sally Jane (Gaskins) O'Neal, Armeda (Garrish) O'Neal, Hilda (Tolson) McWilliams, Edith (O'Neal) Simpson and Susan (Fulcher) O'Neal. Standing in back, left to right: Bertha (O'Neal) Garrish and Eva Bell (Williams) Williams. The picture dates from around 1910.

CRACOKE N.C.

W. G. Willis Dock & General Mdse. Store, Ocracoke, N. C.

Directions

Walk across the street to the community store shops. A large sign reading Portsmouth Island BOAT TOURS identifies this building. It is okay to walk out on the dock, but be careful.

39. Willis Store and Fish House

Buildings on piers extending into the water were logical constructions for a town that received the vast majority of its goods from freight boats. These buildings served as stores, net houses, fish houses and havens for informal social gatherings. This business was built around 1930 and first operated by Captain Will Willis (Site #38). The mailboats docked here until a pier was built at the post office. Apart from general merchandise, large fuel tanks provided islanders with kerosene and diesel.

In 1958 his son Jack took over the store. Locals and tourists alike have abundant documentation of Jack's Dock, as many 1960s and '70s fishing charters returned here to proudly display their catch.

The store is now home to Annabelle's Florist.

40. (former) Light Plant

Stanley Wahab (Site #6) was instrumental in bringing electricity and many other modern comforts to the island. Due largely to his efforts Ocracoke's first electric generating plant was built in 1936. One must imagine that the vast majority of islanders welcomed refrigeration, radios and fans. The local name for the building was the "ice house" after the luxury for which it was most appreciated. The plant was originally attached to large gas tanks that stood at the end of the Willis' dock (Site #39). The first employees earned $30 a month.

Ocracoke now receives its power from the Tideland Electric Membership Co op, which built a new plant in the 1970s and upgraded in the 1990s to meet the increasing demands of summertime. Many businesses own and operate their own generators, as blackouts occasionally occur during storms or heat waves or when utility lines fail on Hatteras Island. Islanders rarely complain of the inconvenience. Most remember the days of frequent outages, and many recall the flicker of kerosene lamps.

Featured Shopping
- The Community Store   page 84
- The Gathering Place page88
- Village Diva .... page 89
- Captain's Cargo .... page 89

Directions
When you walk back off the docks the Site 40 is on your left.

Featured Shopping
- Joyces of Ocracoke ..... page 87

Featured Accommodation
- Joyce's of Ocracoke Motel & Dockage page107
- Harborside Motel .... page 106
- Anchorage Inn .... page 106

Photo Cred t: Ann Ehringhaus

The former light plant has gone through many incarnations. It housed Willis' Store in this photo from the 1970s.

Mending the nets.

Directions:

To return to the tour's beginning, take a left out of the Community Store parking lot. Stay on Highway 12 until you reach the large parking lot. Thanks for taking the time to find out more about Ocracoke and some of the people who choose to live here. We hope you were able to envision life on the island as it used to be. Even in the heat and hubbub of summertime the past can still be seen and felt.

This book should not be mistaken for a comprehensive history. Anyone interested in the history of the island and tenor of its people will find Alton Ballance's *Ocracokers* invaluable. Historical records researched and compiled by Ellen Fulcher Cloud are available for sale in the Ocracoke Preservation Society Museum Gift Shop, as are her well-documented books. Ann Ehringhaus' *Ocracoke Portrait* offers an often stirring portrayal, in words and photos, of the island's spirit. All three are local authors. *The Waterman's Song: Slavery and Freedom in Maritime North Carolina* by David Cecelski is a fascinating read which illuminates the whole of colonial and pre-Civil War coastal society. And the classic *Ocracoke* by Carl Goerch makes everyone that loves Ocracoke happy and a bit wistful. 🐾

Ocracoke Island Now ✦

Visiting Ocracoke Island Today

Getting Around

Ocracoke can no longer properly be called a quaint fishing village. Though plenty of fishing happens in local waters, the economy now centers around tourism. Summers bustle with people and activity. Traveling by foot or bike is the way to get the most out of island life, though boats, of course, play a prominent role.

Ferries from Hatteras Island run continuously throughout the summer season; wait times may average 1-2 hours. If you're day-tripping from the north during the high season it might be wise to make friends in the ferry line and share the 13-mile ride to the village. Reservations can be made for both the Cedar Island (800-856-0343) and Swan Quarter (800-773-1094) ferries, which travel from the south and west, respectively..

In spite of its remote location, Ocracoke has services and amenities similar to other small American towns. There is a gas station, garage, several grocers, a liquor store, hardware store, bank, health clinic, volunteer fire department, public K-12 school, two Protestant churches, a Catholic congregation and a Quaker meeting, a day care facility, a weekly and a monthly newspaper and a library. Visitors will find restaurants to suit many tastes, a variety of hotels and inns, gift shops and a handful of bars. (First-time visitors should know that bars and restaurants on

Ocracoke are only licensed to serve wine and beer.)

Work for most islanders relates to tourism. Many people own and operate small businesses; others work on the ferries or as servers, clerks, cleaners, cooks, boat captains, Realtors, plumbers, electricians, landscapers, carpenters, hunting guides, house painters, massage therapists, fishermen, web designers, waste disposers, teachers and nurses. It is not uncommon for an islander to have two or more jobs in the summer, and locals are disinclined to attach status to employment. The person who cleaned your cottage may teach high school during the winter, and a classically trained musician may be bagging your groceries.

The year-round population is around 770. People choose to live here for the homemade music and pot-luck suppers, the natural beauty, the thrum of summer-time, the quiet of winter and because it's home and always has been. Islanders feel strongly connected to their history, their people, the land and water. Living well on Ocracoke means sharing fish and fish stories, helping a neighbor prepare for a hurricane, gossip in the grocery aisle, grieving together when a community member dies, dressing up for the Fourth of July parade, starry cold winter nights and knowing how to fix your own plumbing.

Visitors who don't mind a few bugs and appreciate solitude and self-suffi-ciency will find much to enjoy on Ocracoke. The pace of island life has quickened in the past few decades, but the ethos of independence and humor that served earlier generations remains.

Services

Annabelle's Florist and Antiques

Community Store Square on the pier, N.C. Hwy. 12   (252)928-4541

Islander Chester Lynn has long been locally recognized as a gifted floral decorator, and now his services are available to the public. Working out of a unique historic structure on a dock in the harbor, Lynn creates arrangements for birthdays, funerals, holidays and other occasions, or no occasion at all. The store also sells antiques and gifts.

Cheryl Roberts

(252)928-7143

Violinist Cheryl Roberts hits just the right note for weddings but is available to enhance other occasions as well. Her repertoire features a variety of classical songs. Her musical stylings must be booked in advance.

East Carolina Bank

N.C. Hwy. 12   (252)928-5231

East Carolina Bank is a full-service bank located across the street from the Pony Island Motel, next door to the Flying Melon. There is a 24-hour ATM machine at this location.

Ice Pirate Prints

Island Girl Gift Shop, Back Road
(252)928-3404

Design your own vacation T-shirts and proudly wear them home. Commemorate family reunions, weddings, a great fishing trip or a hedonistic beach vacation with friends. There's a minimum order of 12.

Island Path Workshops and Seminars

The Lightkeeper's Guest House, Creek Road   (877) 708-7284

Through workshops, seminars and retreats, Island Path is dedicated to helping people reach their full potential. The guides describe the retreats as journeys for change and for becoming the person of your dreams. Island Path offers Personal Path Retreat Weeks, where you are given time to reflect on your life and to address the changes that need to be made. A personal retreat also nourishes the creative spirit and offers healing and support for life transitions. Personal Path Retreats are unique to the participants; you can come alone or with others, and you tell the guide what course you would like to take. Island Path also offers six-day camps for writers, titled The Complete Writer: Combining Business and Creativity for Writing Success. The camps are intensive, with 16 hours of scheduled class time, 14 hours of writing, one-on-one mentoring plus recreational activities like t'ai chi, massage, beach-going and biking. Four writers camps are held each year. Ruth Fordon, co-founder of Island Path, is also a Mentor Coach and offers personal coaching.

Beach Towing and Wrecker Service

(252)928-6160 or (252)928-3720

It happens. Beach Towing is the island's AAA contact and Jesse Spencer is the man to call if your keys are locked in the car or your vehicle is stuck. He will get you straight without making you feel silly and offers free beach driving tips with each tow.

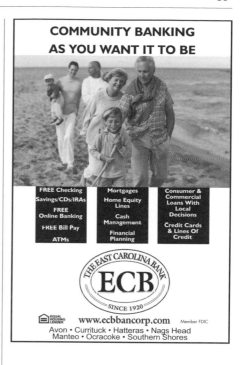

Halo Hair Studio

58 Creek Road   (252)588-0000

Freshen up yourself and your look at Halo Hair Studio. The delightful owner Susie Kennedy personally handles all the cuts and coloring. The salon features spa products and quality vegan shampoos and conditioners. They work by appointment, and wedding parties are welcomed.

Jimmy's Garage

Ocean View Road, behind the Pony Island Motel   (252)928-6603

This full-service garage receives accolades from vacationers who've experienced car trouble. Demand can be high in the summer time, and Jimmy's is the island's only official repair shop, but this family-run business will get you back on the road as soon as they possibly can.

Ocracoke Child Care, Inc.
Old Beach Road
(behind Captain Ben's Restaurant)
(252)928-4131

The motto at this caring, highly rated facility is "Peace Begins on the Play-ground." Open Monday-Friday from 7:45 am-5:15 pm, child care is available to tourists by the day, half day or hour. Call to check availability.

Pelican Airways
(252)928-1661 or 1-888-7PELICAN

New since 2004 are scheduled flights in-season to and from both Norfolk, VA, and Beaufort, NC. One-way trips cost $79 on the Beaufort leg and $129 on the Norfolk route. Round-trip tickets are somewhat cheaper. Charters to anywhere are available, and Pelican Airways' experienced pilot specializes in exotic destinations. Sightseeing tours over Ocracoke and Portsmouth are also available, as is flying instruction.

Sandy Paws Bed & Biscuit Inn
West End Road   (252)928-3093

If you can't bear to leave your animals at home but your rental cottage or motel doesn't allow pets, Sandy Paws is the answer. This is a boarding kennel and day care for cats and dogs. West End Road is on the north end of town just before the ABC store and Community Center.

Tuff as Nails
94 ½ British Cemetery Road, Down the lane that is across the street from Island Artworks   (252)928-7069

Tuff as Nails offers manicures, pedicures and soothing paraffin waxes in a sunny, artful building behind the proprietor's home. Choices include acrylics, silks, gels and airbrushing. Wednesdays are open to drop-ins, otherwise appointments are necessary. Wedding parties are welcome.

Ocracoke Health Center
Back Road   (252)928-1511
After hours   (252)928-7425
Emergencies   911

Recently expanded, the Health Center has provided care to the sick and wounded since the early 1980s. EMTs are always on call, and appointments can be made for office visits.

Ocracoke Library
Back Road,
across from Ocracoke Coffee Co.
(252)928-4436

Part of the Beaufort-Hyde Regional Libraries, the Ocracoke Library offers a rotating selection of books and periodicals, internet access, Thursday night scrabble and a wide porch full of rocking chairs.

Quay Haul Productions
Spencer's Market, corner of N.C. Hwy 12 and School Rd.   (252) 928-1410

Jerry Ricks artfully communicates using new media. He can provide computer technical support and services such as digital printing and photo enhancement. Ask about web design, photography and internet marketing or media projects like creating a film or website about your vacation. Call for an appointment.

Marine Services

A public boat ramp is located at the northwestern end of the National Park Service parking lot, near the Cedar Island and Swan Quarter ferry terminals. Personal watercraft (i.e. Waverunners and Jet Skis) cannot be launched from public land. The Anchorage Marina and Harborside Motel both have boat ramps that may be used for a small fee.

Fuel is available at the Anchorage Marina and the Community Store docks. The Anchorage has a pump-out station, and Sea Tow operates a boat out of Ocracoke during the warmer months.

Transient docking is available at the National Park Service docks, Anchorage Marina and sometimes at the Community Store docks.

A dinghy dock is on the wharf at the Community Store. When approaching from the water, it is to the right of the pier.

Boaters needing repairs may find guidance from the staff at the Anchorage Marina.

Ocracoke Island Weddings

An Ocracoke marriage will have both an intimate setting and a vast, sparkling horizon. The island's unique geography makes it a special place; it can also create challenges, as not all services available in mainland towns are to be found on Ocracoke. Know that an island wedding may require flexibility. After a storm knocked out power lines, one couple found themselves marrying by candlelight. Dancing to acoustic music in the flickering light made it all the more magical.

There are two churches on the island and a community center available for rent, though many couples find other venues suit their needs. Some rent soundfront cottages or condos for use as reception sites. For small wedding parties, getting married on Pamlico Sound aboard a schooner is an option.

It is of course also possible to be wed on the beach or on the lighthouse grounds. Special Use Permits can be obtained for $100 from the Cape Hatteras National Seashore (252) 473-2111 ext. 121. Any NC Register of Deeds Office can issue a marriage license for $50. The Hyde County office is in Swan Quarter (252) 926-4198.

A number of island restaurants are willing to cater, though tents and chairs cannot be rented on the island. There are talented local musicians and floral decorators to make the day of your dreams wonderful.

Ocracoke Occasions
Firefly Gift Shop, Sunset Drive
(a.k.a. Firehouse Road)
(252)928-3401

Planning a wedding or other event on Ocracoke? Ocracoke Occasions can ease your burden. Local resident Nancy Leach knows what and who is happening on the island as well as where and how to facilitate the event you're dreaming of. But she needs time to work her magic; call in advance. ☙

Wedding Resources

Clergy

Assembly of God .... (252) 928-9001
Catholic .... (252) 928-1661/3543
United Methodist .... (252) 928-4211
Nondenominational .... (252) 928-7245

Magistrates

Lonnie Burrus .... (252) 928-5381
John Fletcher .... (252) 928-4135

Caterers

Back Porch Restaurant ... (252) 928-6401
Café Atlantic .... (252) 928-4861
Capt. Ben's Restaurant ... (252) 928-4741
Creekside Café .... (252) 928-3606
Jason's Restaurant .... (252) 928-3434
Martelle's Catering .... (252) 925-1799
Pelican Restaurant .... (252) 928-7431
Sargasso Deepwater Grill .. (252) 928-2874
sMacNally's .... (252) 928-9999

Florists

Annabelle's Florist .... (252) 928-4541
Flowers at Silver Lake ..... (252) 928-3086
Sally Newell Interiors ..... (252) 928-6141

Hair Stylists

Halo Hair Studio .... (252) 588-0000

Spa Services & Massage

Deep Blue Day Spa .... (252) 921-0182
Massage Therapy & Reiki (252) 928-1311
Ocracoke Massage .... (252) 928-5801
Tuff as Nails .... (252) 928-7069

Jewelers

Barbara Hardy Jewelry ..... (252) 928-6793
Island Artworks .... (252) 928-3892

Musicians

Cheryl Roberts .... (252) 928-7143
Coyote .... (252) 928-9975
Jamie Tunnell .... (252) 928-2679

Martin Garrish .... (252) 928-4751
Molasses Creek .... (252) 928-4280

Photographers/Videograhpers

Trudy Austin .... (252) 928-3781
Ann Ehringhaus .... (252) 928-1311
Jennifer Garrish .... (252) 928-4301
Clayton Gaskill .... (252) 928-7491
Quay Haul Productions ... (252) 928-1410

Wedding Cake Bakers

Fig Tree Bakery .... (252) 928-4554
Ronnie Ciccone .... (252) 928-4703

Wedding Coordinators

Ocracoke Occasions .... (252) 928-3401
Ocracoke Concierge .... (252) 928-6655
Schooner Windfall .... (252) 928-SAIL

HISTORIC LIGHTHOUSE, OCRACOKE ISLAND, NORTH CAROLINA

Ocracoke Island Attractions ❧

Most of Ocracoke Island's attractions are of the best variety: free! Or at least they're very inexpensive. The attractions here are simple and unfettered, with few of the usual commercial trappings of a tourist site. There are no go-cart tracks, mini-golf courses, waterslides or movie theaters. On Ocracoke, the island itself is an attraction. When people are here, they just don't need as much stimulation. Quiet walks on the beach, fishing and clamming, looking for shells, building a sandcastle, strolling around the village, sitting on the porch swing, observing nature or chasing ghost crabs in the moonlight: These are the simple attractions on Ocracoke Island. For a little extra entertainment, bike over to the lighthouse and the Preservation Museum, or go out and visit the ponies and take a little hike. You get the idea.

The Beach

The top attraction on the island is, of course, the beach. What makes Ocracoke's oceanside extremely inviting is that there is absolutely no development, save for a couple of public access ramps and a public campground. This is part of the Cape Hatteras National Seashore, forever protected from development and one of the most beautiful and pristine stretches of beach you'll find anywhere.

There are several ways to get on the beach. Nine ramps allow for easy crossover from N.C. Highway 12 to the beach. Five of them provide access for four-wheel-drive vehicles. Driving is allowed on Ocracoke's beaches, so if you have a four-wheel-drive vehicle you can drive right out and claim a section of beach as yours for the day. Be sure to inform yourself of beach-driving tips, and do not attempt to drive on the beach in a two-wheel-drive vehicle. Four-wheel-drive ramps are: Ramp 72 just south of the Airstrip, Ramp 70 at the Airstrip, Ramp 68 at the National Park Service Campground, Ramp 67 north of the Campground, and Ramp 59 at the northernmost tip of the island near the Hatteras ferry docks. Parking areas and walkover ramps are available at several places on the island.

If you prefer swimming near a lifeguard, which is always a good idea here, the National Park Service stations a lifeguard north of Ramp 70, the first parking area past the Airstrip. Lifeguards are on duty from Memorial Day through Labor Day.

National Park Service Ocracoke Island Visitor Center

N.C. Hwy. 12   (252) 928-4531

The majority of land on Ocracoke is part of the Cape Hatteras National Seashore and is publicly owned and administered by the National Park Service. The island's NPS Visitor Center is at the southernmost end of N.C. 12 near the Cedar Island and Swan Quarter ferry docks. The center is a clearinghouse for all types of island and national seashore information. You'll find an information desk, helpful staff, a bookshop, free maps and informational brochures and exhibits about the island. Inquire here about the Park Service's boat docks and special ranger-led programs. The visitor center is open March through December.

Historic Marker of Fort Ocracoke

N.C. Hwy. 12, behind the NPS Visitor Center

This marker is a little hard to find, but it's worth seeking out. It's on a grassy patch behind the National Park Service Visitor Center and next to the boat ramp. Park the car and walk out to the sound and you'll see it. The marker commemorates Fort Ocracoke, the remnants of which lie

submerged in Ocracoke Inlet toward Portsmouth Island. The fort was constructed by volunteers beginning on May 20, 1861, the day North Carolina seceded from the Union to join the Confederacy. One side of the marker lists all of the men from Ocracoke and Portsmouth islands who were killed in the Civil War.

Ocracoke Preservation Society and Museum

N.C. Hwy. 12   (252) 928-7375

For a peek into Ocracoke's past, visit Ocracoke Preservation Society's Museum. Housed in the turn-of-the-century home of Coast Guard Capt. David Williams (see the Walking Tour section of this book), the museum lets visitors glimpse island life in the early to mid-1900s. Many of the original architectural elements are still intact, and a bedroom, living room and kitchen are decorated with period furnishings donated by locals. The museum has photographs, artifacts and exhibits that pertain to island life and culture. There's a small gift shop as well. Upstairs is a small research library that can be used with permission. It's free to visit the museum, though donations are encouraged. It's open from Easter through the end of November.

British Cemetery

British Cemetery Road

On May 11, 1942, about 40 miles south of Ocracoke, a German submarine torpedoed and sank the British vessel HMS Bedfordshire. The 170-foot ship was one of 24 antisubmarine ships loaned to the United States by Winston Churchill. The entire crew of four officers and 33 crewmen

Please Join the Ocracoke Preservation Society

You are invited to become a member of the Ocracoke Preservation Society. Money from memberships, donations and memorials is used to operate our museum and fund special projects.

Individual, Family, Honorary, and Business Memberships run from January through December of each year.
Send your name, address, phone number and check to:
Ocracoke Preservation Society • P. O. Box 1240• Ocracoke, NC 27960

TYPE OF MEMBERSHIPS:

$ 15 INDIVIDUAL – 1 year
$ 30 FAMILY – 1 year
$ 50 HONORARY – 1 year
$ 100 BUSINESS – 1 year

$ 500 SUSTAINING –
   5 years for a business
   10 years for an individual/family
$1000 LIFETIME

---

drowned. U.S. Coast Guard officers found four of the bodies washed ashore three days later. The soldiers were buried on a plot of land next to a family's cemetery on land donated to Britain. The Coast Guard still maintains the grave sites and flies a British flag over the graves. Every year on the anniversary of the sailors' deaths, there is a ceremony to honor the British sailors. The adjacent village cemetery also provides an interesting look back into Ocracoke Island's past.

Ocracoke Lighthouse
Lighthouse Road

Ocracoke Lighthouse may the shortest of the four Outer Banks lighthouses but that only makes it all the more charming. About 70 feet tall, the white-washed tower sits on a lawn of flawless green surrounded by a white picket fence, outbuildings and a quaint keeper's cottage, creating a picturesque scene of old island life. Built in 1823, this is the oldest lighthouse in North Carolina and the second oldest in the nation. It is still in operation, and its beam

See www.OcracokeGuide.com for full content, links & updates.

can be seen 14 miles out to sea. The lighthouse is not open for tours or climbing, but you can walk down the boardwalk leading to it to get an up-close view. Volunteers are sometimes on site to answer questions.

Deepwater Theater
Schoolhouse Road   (252) 928-4280

Deepwater Theater is the home theater of Molasses Creek, Ocracoke Island's hometown band that's built a loyal following with its blend of soulful singing, bluegrass fiddlin' and occasionally skewed sense of humor. From June through August, Molasses Creek plays here on Tuesday and Thursday evenings. On Wednesday evenings the Ocrafolk Opry takes over, featuring a panoply of local musicians and special visiting guests. Shows begin at 8:30 p.m. Get there by 8 p.m. to assure yourself a seat. The theater is actually a small, enclosed screened porch, so there's limited seating available. Ticket prices are around $12 for adults and $6 for children.

Ocracoke Pony Pens
N.C. Hwy. 12

There are many theories about how ponies found their way to Ocracoke Island. Some say they arrived on English ships during 16th-century exploration, others say they were victims of Spanish shipwrecks, and some say they were simply livestock for the locals. However they got here, the ponies roamed the island freely for at least

two centuries and were very much a part of the island lifestyle in days gone by. The local Boy Scouts even rode them, making them the only mounted troop in the country.

When N.C. 12 was paved in 1957, cars and ponies began to collide. The National Park Service wanted to get rid of the entire herd, but the islanders protested and the Park Service agreed to contain some of the ponies on the island. In 1959, they developed the Ocracoke Pony Pens, a 180-acre pasture area that today houses about 30 ponies. Several ponies are rotated up to the front pasture so that visitors can always get a look at these unusual equines. The Ocracoke ponies have distinctive physical characteristics: five lumbar vertebrae instead of the six found in most horses, 17 ribs instead of 18 and a unique shape, posture, color, size and weight.

The pens are located on N.C. 12 about 7 miles north of the village. It's free to visit, but donations are welcome to help pay for the food and veterinary care of the ponies. Remember: The ponies are not tame, and they may try to kick or bite you if you try to feed or touch them.

Hammock Hills Nature Trail
N.C. Hwy. 12

Just across from the National Park Service's Ocracoke Campground, the Hammock Hills Nature Trail is a 3/4-mile trail through the island's maritime forest and salt marsh. It's a great trail for nature lovers and bird-watchers, and there are informative signposts along the way. The hike takes about 30 minutes.

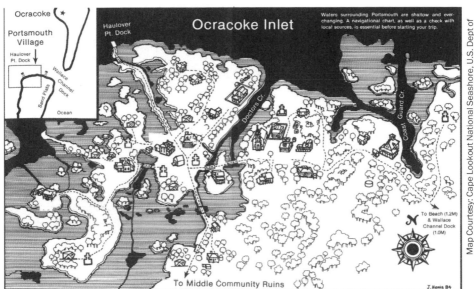

A map of Portsmouth Village.

Portsmouth Island

Portsmouth Island, just across the inlet from Ocracoke Island, is an enchanting place to visit. This uninhabited island is rugged and remote, one of the last Atlantic coast islands that is free of development, thanks to its status as part of the Cape Lookout National Seashore. There is much to do on this island, all of it free and simple, filled with history and the allure of the natural world.

On the north end of the island is a veritable ghost town known as Portsmouth Village. The village was once one of the largest settlements on the Outer Banks, though no one lives there now, save a caretaker. Portsmouth Village was established in 1753 on the shores of Ocracoke

Inlet, and it was predominantly a "lightering" village. Large ships that used Ocracoke Inlet as a major trade route to the mainland would have to be unloaded to pass through the inlet and the shallow sounds and then reloaded as they found deeper waters. The residents of Portsmouth Village did the lightering of the load by moving goods to several smaller flatboats and then reloading the ships a ways down the water. A large community sprang up around this business, with a post office, a church, a school and many homes.

In 1846 Hatteras Inlet opened in a hurricane and was deeper and safer than Ocracoke Inlet. The shipping route shifted to the north, and the Portsmouth villagers had to find other ways to make a living. Later, during the Civil War, many islanders fled to the mainland to avoid advancing Union troops and never came back after the war. Portsmouth Village's population

An excursion to Portsmouth Village is well worth the effort.

continued to decline until there were only three residents left in 1970. In 1971, one of them died and the other two left the island reluctantly. In 1976 Portsmouth Village was saved when Cape Lookout National Seashore was established. The village is now on the National Register of Historic Places.

Many of the buildings have been restored, and visitors can enter the church, Coast Guard station, schoolhouse and post office for a peek at old island life. The interiors look as if the people have just left, and you can look into the windows of some old buildings and see the villagers' former belongings. There is also a visitor center in a restored house where you'll find restrooms and exhibits on the island's history. You can walk from the village to the beach, though it is a long walk so be prepared. The beach at Portsmouth Island is expansive and clean, and the shelling is outstanding.

Conveniences are few on Portsmouth Island. Restrooms are available, but drinking water and food are not. Bring your own, plus sunscreen and insect repellent. The mosquitoes are voracious on Portsmouth Island. The island is only accessible by boat. See our Recreation chapter for information on Portsmouth Island ferry services and boat rentals. 🐚

Ocracoke Island Recreation ✱✿

Looking for something to do on Ocracoke Island? You won't have trouble finding fun here. From an air tour to a fishing trip to a kayak tour, there are numerous recreational opportunities available that will help you get to know this island and its people a little better.

Air Tours

Pelican Airways
Ocracoke Airstrip
N.C. Hwy. 12   (252) 928-1661

Sightseeing tours (at $49 per person), charters and flying lessons are available from Pelican Airways, which also offers regularly scheduled flights to Norfolk, VA, and Beaufort, NC.

Bicycle & Equipment Rental

Slushy Stand
N.C. Hwy. 12   (252) 928-1878

The Slushy Stand rents adult and kid bikes by the hour, day or week. It's at the corner of N.C. Hwy. 12 and Silver Lake Drive.

Beach Outfitters
N.C. Hwy. 12   (252) 928-6261

Beach Outfitters is located at Ocracoke Island Realty. They rent bikes, beach chairs, umbrellas, boogie boards and appliances too cumbersome to pack, like televisions and grills.

Shore Gear
N.C. Hwy. 12   (252) 928-7060

Shore Gear is located at Sandy Shores Realty. They rent bicycles for kids and adults and also rent beach gear and other vacation items.

Boat Rentals

Restless Native Boat Rentals
Anchorage Marina
N.C. Hwy. 12 (252) 928-1421 or 921-0011

Restless Native rents flat-bottom Carolina Skiffs and Privateers with outboard motors. The owner can give you a brief course in small boat handling and tips about navigating the sound. Boats range in length from 16 to 24 feet. Daily, three-day and weekly packages are available.

Island Boat Rentals
Ocracoke Harbor Inn
Silver Lake Drive   (252) 928-5480

There is nothing quite like spending a sunny day on the water. Island Rentals rents flat-bottom boats ranging from 16 to 19 feet. Boats can be rented by the half-day, day or week.

Boat Tours *Windfall II*

Windfall *Once Stand on 5:00*
Community Square Docks
(252) 928-SAIL (7245)

The Windfall is a traditional gaff-rigged schooner that offers several hour-long day cruises past the lighthouse and Teach's Hole, where Blackbeard was killed. It costs about $20 for adults and $10 for children younger than 12; children younger than 3 sail for free. Longer sunset trips cost a bit more. While this is not a narrated tour, the informed, engaging captain and mate tell stories and happily answer questions. The boat can sail with up to 30 passengers, and reservations are recommended. A second gaff-rigged schooner was recently added to their fleet, and the vessels are available for private charters and weddings.

Miss Ocracoke Sunset Dolphin Cruise
GunBarrell Point Marina, junction of N.C. Hwy. 12 and
Silver Lake Drive   (252) 928-6060

The Miss Ocracoke is a head boat that offers fishing trips and dolphin cruises. The sunset dolphin cruise is held on Tuesday, Wednesday and Thursday at 6:30 p.m. All ages, but especially kids, will enjoy cruising the sound waters looking for the frolicking dolphins. Reservations are recommended.

Photo Credit: Michael McOwen

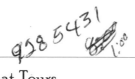

Island Boat Tours

Community Square Docks
N.C. Hwy. 12   (252) 928-4361

Knowledgeable islander Rudy Austin runs a 60- to 90-minute boat tour of the surrounding islands, during which passengers stay on the boat. This tour includes views of Pelican Island and other islands, the lighthouse, the site of Fort Ocracoke and, oftentimes, dolphins. The price is $20 per person with a minimum of four passengers. Regular trips run in spring, summer and fall. Winter trips are on demand. Reservations are recommended.

Charter Boats

Anchorage Marina

N.C. Hwy. 12   (252) 928-6661

To charter a boat to take you fishing offshore in the Gulf Stream, look to Anchorage Marina. Three charter boats operate from here — the Devereaux, Drumstick and Restless — charging about $450 for a half day of fishing and up to $900 for a full day. Each charter accommodates six people, and they can arrange for you to combine parties if you don't have enough people. Some inshore chartering is available here as well. Make reservations in advance.

Fish Tale

(252) 921-0224 or (252) 928-3403

Captain John Ferrara has more than 10 years of experience specializing in light-tackle, inshore trips for families with children. Groups spend two, four or eight hours on the waters of Pamlico Sound catching flounder, red drum, trout, bluefish and Spanish mackerel. All tackle, bait and ice are included as is fish cleaning. Call to check rates and availability.

Gecko

(252) 928-5561

Aboard a comfortable 46-foot custom Carolina boat, Captain Ernest Doshier heads to offshore or inshore waters for full or half days of fishing. You can drop your line in the sloughs of Pamlico Sound or the Gulf Stream. Families are welcome. Bait, tackle and fish-cleaning are included, so you can dine that night on what you caught that day.

Miss Kathleen

Community Square Docks
N.C. Hwy. 12   (252) 928-4841
                           or (800) 305-1472

The Miss Kathleen is a modern vessel with the appeal of a traditional work boat. Native islander Captain Ronnie O'Neal has spent much of his life in the waters around Ocracoke. Both those baiting their first-ever hook and seasoned sports fishermen will benefit from Capt. O'Neal's 30+ years of experience. The Miss Kathleen can be chartered for half- or full-day trips, inshore or off, and provided are all tackle and bait, freezer service and fish cleaning. Single anglers can be accommodated. Be sure to call ahead.

Miss Teresa

(252) 928-7835

Get schooled by Albert O'Neal, the Captain of the Miss Teresa and an island native from a family of fishermen. His wealth of local knowledge and gentle manner will benefit inshore fishermen and fisher-families in search of red drum, sea bass, cobia, flounder and other tasty delights. Full- or half-day charters include ice, bait, tackle, fish-cleaning, anecdotes and tips.

Rascal

Ocracoke Harbor Inn
144 Silver Lake Road (252) 928-6111

Both inshore (half or full day) and offshore (full day) trips are available through Captain Norman Miller, who will equip and educate visitors about wreck, bottom or fly fishing. The Rascal boasts impressive catches of red drum, but local Captain Miller also knows where and how to find other inshore fish. Head off-shore for a full day and hook grouper, snapper, amberjack, dolphin (mahi mahi), barracuda, triggerfish or king mackerel. Lodging and fishing packages are available through the Ocracoke Harbor Inn.

Tarheel

Community Square Docks
N.C. Hwy. 12 (252) 928-9966
or (800) 305-1472

Captain Ryan O'Neal is one of the newest generation of charter boat captains, and he already has his share of citation fish to brag about. He offers full- or half-day inshore charters geared toward families. Tackle, bait and fish cleaning are included in the fee. Have fun while experiencing the way islanders put supper on the table by booking the Tarheel for clamming or a nighttime flounder giggin' trip.

Portsmouth Island Trips

Portsmouth Island, just south of Ocracoke Island, makes for an incredible day trip. On the island you can explore the historic deserted village and remote beaches. Shelling, swimming, fishing, bird watching and hiking are enjoyed here in relative solitude. It takes about 20 minutes by boat to get to Portsmouth Island. There are two businesses that make regular trips: One is a guided tour that uses ATVs as transportation, and the other drops you off and lets you walk around. You can also rent motor boats or kayaks to get there. Nothing is for sale on the island, so you must take everything with you. Bring water, food, sunscreen and insect repellent.

Portsmouth Island ATV Excursions

N.C. Hwy. 12 (252) 928-1184

This outfit ferries passengers to Portsmouth Island for four-hour guided ATV (four-wheeled all-terrain vehicle) excursions, either from 8 a.m. to noon or 2 to 6 p.m. The ATVs accommodate two people, and drivers must be at least 16. Children must be at least 6 to take the tour. Tours cost $75 per person, and the maximum number of passenger is six. Make reservations in advance.

Portsmouth Island Boat Tours

Community Square Docks
N.C. Hwy. 12 (252) 928-4361

Rudy Austin ferries passengers to Portsmouth Island. He drops them off at the historic village with a self-guided tour map and then picks them up on the beach about four hours later. The first boat leaves at 9:30 a.m., with pickup at 2 p.m. If there is demand, a second boat leaves at 11 a.m., with pickup at 3:30 p.m. The price is $20 per person. Austin also runs a 60- to 90-minute boat tour of the surrounding

You can rent Waverunners by the hour or half-hour on Ocracoke Island.

Photo Credit: Michael McOwen

islands; see the Boat Tours section. Regular trips run in spring, summer and fall. Winter trips are on demand. Reservations are recommended.

Watersports

Parasailing

GunBarrell Point Marina, junction of
N.C. Hwy 12 and
Silver Lake Drive   (252) 921-2606

Parasailing combines stunning views with the thrill of flying high above Pamlico Sound. This locally owned operation runs trips throughout the day, or you can call ahead for an appointment.

Ride the Wind Surf Shop

N.C. Hwy. 12   (252) 928-6311

To see another side of Ocracoke Island, take a kayak ecotour with Ride the Wind. They offer guided sunrise, midday and sunset tours for up to 10 people. On a tour, you are provided with the kayak, a paddle, a life vest, a dry bag in which to put your camera and other gear, a net, a field guide, a human guide and any training you

need. Ride the Wind also rents kayaks by the hour, day or week; you can choose from sit-on-top, sit-in, touring or surf kayaks. The folks at this shop also offer a great Surf Camp for ages 9 to 13 that includes surfing, surf kayaking, body boarding and kayak touring. The three-day camp is held from 1 to 4 p.m. on Tuesday, Wednesday and Thursday. If adults want to do this, you can arrange for a special family camp. Make reservations for both the kayak tours and surf camps.

Ocracoke Adventures

N.C. Hwy. 12   (252) 928-7873

These outfitters offers kayak ecotours in the Pamlico Sound and strive to make its paddlers more aware of the fragile ecology of the environment they are visiting. Several daily ecotours are offered, including an early morning tour, a tour of Blackbeard's domain, a sunset tour and a full-moon tour, among others. Tours are guided by biologists and last about two to two and a half hours. The fee includes the kayak, paddle, backrest, life jacket, dry bag, instructions and the guide. Customized educational tours are available. Kayaks can

be rented for individual paddling by the hour, day and week. Ocracoke Adventures also offers a summer Wave Cave surf camp for children that includes surfing lessons, body boarding and surf kayaking. Call to make reservations.

Ocracoke Wave Runners

GunBarrell Point Marina, junction of N.C. Hwy. 12 and
Silver Lake Drive   (252) 928-2600, (252) 588-0011 or (252) 588-0012

Wave Runners allow you to experience the waters between Ocracoke and Portsmouth at the helm of a maneuverable, fun and speedy vessel. Riders must be at least 18 to pilot, or 16 with an accompanying parent or guardian. Each Wave Runner carries up to two people. Rentals are by the hour or half hour.

Hunting

Ocracoke Waterfowl Hunting
(252) 928-5751

Ocracoke Waterfowl Hunting provides a unique site for waterfowl hunters. With 4' by 8' bushed blinds available, there is no better way to get close to the various types of waterfowl around Pamlico Sound. Native islander Monroe Gaskill, a licensed guide, has been showing hunters the best locations for more than 16 years. Hunting has been a part of his family for more than three generations. Gaskill provides transportation to the blinds, places for dogs to rest and a full rig of more than 100 decoys per blind. Hunting seasons vary. Reservations are recommended.

Open Water Duck Hunting
(252) 928-7170

Fourth generation island guide Wade Austin offers up to six hunters the opportunity to take aim at red heads, widgeons, pintails, blue bills, brants, geese, black duck and more. Hunters are accommodated by either curtain boxes or stake blinds. Open Water Duck Hunting assures transportation to and from the blinds, furnishes decoys and can arrange for lodging.

Island Guide Services
(252) 928-2504 or (252) 928-2509

Licensed guides Kenneth Tillett and Earl Gaskins both have 19 years of experience, hunting expertise and local knowledge. Tillett's great-grandfather, Charlie McWilliams, and Gaskins' grandfather, Thurston Gaskill, both led parties for the Green Island Hunting Club. Island Guide Services continues the tradition, offering stake and pit blinds, decoys and transport.

Russell Williams
(252) 928-4408

Williams is a licensed guide with more than 12 years of experience who has appeared in both Wildfowl and Carolina Adventure magazines. He transports hunters to curtain blinds or sink boxes, a type of blind developed on Pamlico Sound and legal only in Hyde and Dare counties. Reservations should be made before Thanksgiving, and packages including accommodation can be arranged through the Pony Island Motel.

Massage and Spa

Deep Blue Day Spa
At the Castle B&B
Silver Lake Drive   (252) 921-0182

Licensed massage therapists Amy Borland and Laura Curry (formerly of Live Oak Massage) offer services to restore your mind, body and spirit. They offer a variety of therapy styles, including Swedish, connective tissue, craniosacral, ocean stone and Yogassage. Spa services include facials, dry-body brushing, paraffin therapy and Thalassotherapy. The spa services are very popular, so it's recommended that you make appointments well in advance.

Massage Therapy and Reiki
N.C. Hwy. 12   (252) 928-1311

Ann Ehringhaus, a N.C.-licensed massage therapist, offers Chinese acupressure, Rosen method emotional bodywork and Reiki sessions and classes. Ann, who has a M.Ed. in counseling and is a Reiki master, did much of her bodywork studying in Berkeley, California, and Chapel Hill. Her office is next door to Oscar's House B&B, which she operates.

Ocracoke Massage
(252) 928-5801

Licensed massage therapists Cindy Fiore and Carolyn Wynn offer therapeutic massage on Ocracoke Island. Choose from Swedish massage, acupressure massage, craniosacral massage, neuromuscular therapy and acupressure facials. Appointments are available Monday through Saturday.

Fitness

Hatha Yoga
Deepwater Theater
School Road   (252) 921-0182

Local resident Amy Borland offers Hatha yoga classes at Deepwater Theater on School Road throughout the summer. All levels of students are welcome. Call for hours. Cost is $12 for an hour-long class.

Free Workout

Ocracoke Community Center,
N.C. Hwy. 12

Aerobics classes for people of all levels and ages are offered weekday mornings at the Community Center. The days and times are posted on the marquee at the Community Center. The classes are free.

Shopping on Ocracoke is a little different than anywhere else. You can find the best gems down side lanes and paths. This lemonade stand on Howard Street seemed to fit right in.

Ocracoke Island Shopping ❧

Shops on Ocracoke are distinctive and full of character. You won't find the same stuff in store after store as you do in other tourist locations. Many shops feature handcrafted local artwork. The best thing to do is to set out on foot or on a bicycle and just explore. Surprises will await you around every corner of the village. Some of the shops are tucked back off the road, so keep your eyes open for a special find. For the necessities, there are tackle shops, a hardware store and a couple of small community grocery stores. Gas is available on the north end of the village on N.C. Highway 12.

Grocers

The Community Store
Community Square Shops
N.C. Hwy. 12   (252) 928-3321

This harborfront store, in operation since 1918, is a traditional gathering place, and a grocery filled with food staples as well as drinks, snacks, specialty dressings and sauces, household goods, pharmaceuticals and film. Videos can be rented here (two for $4.98), and gas is available for boats on the dock. You can make copies or pay to use the fax machine.

Ocracoke Station
N.C. Hwy. 12   (252) 928-4031

This local gas station and convenience store has recently added a great sandwich counter. Of course, hot coffee, beer, ice, soft drinks, candy and snack items, many necessities and groceries are also still available. You can get propane for your camp stove here, as well as beach supplies and souvenirs.

Ocracoke Variety Store and True Value Hardware
N.C. Hwy. 12   (252) 928-4911

Variety is key at this large one-stop store on the north end of the village. The Variety Store is a grocery store where you'll find produce, meats, beer and wine and almost all of your grocery needs. It's also the place for beach supplies, ice, camping supplies, household items, beauty

products, over-the-counter medicines, gifts, magazines, newspapers and books. The front foyer has a bulletin board and racks containing all sorts of local announcements and advertisements. The True Value Hardware Store is next door, and the ABC (liquor) store is next to that. There is an ATM machine here.

South Point Market
N.C. Hwy. 12
on the harbor   (252) 928-5601
Fresh seafood is sold from the storefront at South Point Seafood, where many local fishermen unload their daily catch.

We'll all miss stopping by Albert Styron's Store for a soda or snack on the porch.
The store is now the home of Village Print. Learn more about the store on page 41.

Sunflower Center

Back Road   (252) 928-6261

The health food store in the Sunflower Center complex carries exclusively organic products, including packaged foods and fresh produce in season. An informed staff can aid your selection of herbal remedies and vitamins.

Sporting Goods

O'Neal's Dockside II

N.C. Hwy. 12   (252) 928-1111

O'Neal's offers a huge selection of bait and tackle and rods and reels. Fishing advice is free, and fishing gear is available for rent. O'Neal's also stocks much-needed camping supplies, boating supplies and beach gear.

Tradewinds Bait & Tackle

N.C. Hwy. 12   (252) 928-5491

There's no question that Ocracoke is an angler's paradise. When you're ready to sink a line, head here for bait, tackle, rod and reel rentals, gear repairs, fishing reports and advice.

Gift Shops, Refreshments & Confections

British Cemetery Road and Vicinity

Over the Moon

British Cemetery Road   (252) 928-3555

This is a fun store, one you'll want to visit again and again. The gifts and crafts are unusual and eclectic. Look for clocks, frames, pottery, jewelry, recycled art, wooden bowls and more contemporary crafts. The whimsical and inspiring Brian Andreas Story People prints and sculptures are sold here.

Island Artworks

British Cemetery Road (252) 928-3892

Island Artworks is a fun place to browse and shop. Owner/artist Kathleen O'Neal sells her own hand-crafted jewelry here, along with blown glass, contemporary crafts, mosaics, photography, watercolors, pottery, woodworks, sculpture, garden accessories and many other works of art. Island artists are well represented.

Photo Credit: Michael McOwen

Candyland

British Cemetery Road (252) 928-4387

When you're out browsing the island shops, nothing will pick you up quicker than a blast of something sweet. Visit Candyland for more than 18 varieties of fresh fudge. Free samples are offered if you can't make up your mind. Believe us, there's some candy or other sweet treat here with your name on it!

Ocracoke Island Hammock Co.

British Cemetery Road (252) 928-4387

A hammock is one of the best vacation souvenirs you can buy: It will remind you to take it easy all year long. You can try out all the hammocks, hammock chairs and porch swings here before you buy them, to assure a perfect fit. The hammocks are made on-site. It's a gift shop too.

Silver Lake Trading Co.

538 Back Road   (252) 928-3086

The owners of this store have an eye for hip, fun, must-have stuff. They're always bringing in new things to add to the eclectic mix, like vintage toys and lunch boxes, pottery, cool works of art, home and garden accessories, frames, lamps, pillows, linens, magnets and just plain kitsch. Customers can always be heard giggling at the silly greeting cards and cocktail napkins.

Silver Lake Harbor (N.C. Hwy. 12)

The Slushy Stand

N.C. Hwy. 12   (252) 928-1878

The Slushy Stand is the place for refreshment. Stop in for ice cream, frozen yogurt, cool slushies, cold drinks and snacks. Relax on the porch and watch the world go by. Bike rentals are available here; see our Recreation section.

Limey's Shave Ice

Next to Anchorage Inn
N.C. Hwy. 12   No phone

Limey was given his nickname when he moved to the island, and, like an American, he's capitalizing on it. Look for the vivid Union Jack, then pick up refreshing shave ice or other frozen goodies to enjoy as you watch boats in the harbor or stroll the village.

Barefoot Bohemian

214 Irvin Garrish Highway
(N.C. 12)   (252) 928-9090

The owners of this new shop have a mantra: "funktacular eclectiscism for the tragically unhip." Barefoot Bohemian

features locally made clothing by Heartwood Designs, bags, candles, beaded curtains, hats, jewelry, fabrics, edgy T-shirts and stickers, handmade soaps and fuzzy knit scarves.

Harborside Gift Shop
N.C. Hwy. 12   (252) 928-3111

An Ocracoke mainstay since 1965, this gift shop across from the Harborside Motel offers brand-name clothing, sportswear, hats, T-shirts, sports gear, batik dresses, gourmet foods and wine, jewelry, sunglasses and gift items.

Joyce's of Ocracoke
N.C. Hwy. 12   (252) 928-6461

This waterfront shop offers sportswear and resort wear for men and women. In addition, Joyce offers collectibles, home accessories, jewelry, gifts, cards, paper products and unique T-shirts.

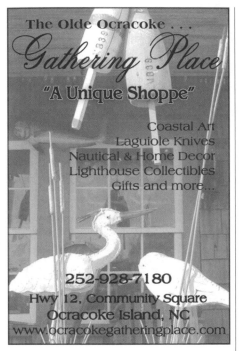

this is the place to come. The selection of kites is enormous, and Ocracoke's wide, uncrowded beach is the perfect place to try out your new purchase. You'll also find flags, beach toys, clothing, shoes, sunglasses and Beanie Babies.

Sunset Sweets
Community Square Shops

Confections and refreshments abound at Sunset Sweets. Homemade fudge and candied apples, frozen yogurt, old-fashioned hard candies, fountain drinks, sundaes, floats and milkshakes can all be enjoyed from the porch while watching the bustle around the harbor.

Up Your Alley

Community Square Shops
N.C. Hwy. 12   (252) 928-5000

You will find men's and women's apparel here that is right up your alley ' dresses and sarongs for women, fashion shirts and more for men. To round things out, there's an interesting selection of handbags, jewelry made by locals, picture frames and votive candles.

Rick's T-Shirt Shop

Community Square Shops
N.C. Hwy. 12   (252) 928-3702

The size of this shop belies its contents. T-shirts for every taste, size and shape abound. Souvenirs and novel gifts are also sold here.

The Gathering Place
N.C. Hwy. 12   (252) 928-7180

This is an inviting shop in a century-old waterfront home. It's stocked with pottery, collectibles, lighthouses and nautical gifts. Visit the upstairs for coastal-

Mermaid's Folly
N.C. Hwy. 12   (252) 928-RAGS

This store stocks items inspired by the sea, including women's fine casual clothing, T-shirts, hats, bags and jewelry.

Island T-Shirts
N.C. Hwy. 12   (252) 928-6781

Sure, you'll find T-shirts at this large souvenir store, but that's not all. You'll also find Ocracoke-themed gifts, nautical items, beach supplies and toys, children's wear, clothing and jewelry. One room is dedicated to Christmas, with many handmade ornaments.

Kitty Hawk Kites

Community Square Shops
N.C. Hwy. 12   (252) 928-4563

Whether you want a simple backyard kite on a string or a sophisticated stunt kite, inspired artwork. If shopping has worn you out, rest awhile on the front porch.

Village Diva

285 Irvin Garrish Highway
(N.C. Hwy. 12)   (252) 928-2828

Women will find much to love in this store, which offers alluring, elegant, comfortable clothing in linen and other natural fabrics, made by companies such as CP Shades and Flax. They sell sun hats and jewelry to complement the clothes and have a selection of home accessories, bath products and yard ornaments.

Captain's Cargo

N.C. Hwy. 12   (252) 928-9991

The newest island shop sells coastal arts and crafts, such as handmade skiffs, whimsical signs, pictures and prints that will be the perfect remembrance of an island vacation. The selection is unique and eclectic.

Downpoint Decoys

N.C. Hwy. 12   (252) 928-3269

This rustic shop is filled to the brim with decoys and sportsman's paraphernalia. The resident carver has been nationally recognized for his work and is a native and can tell you a salty tale or two. There are old and new decoys, lures, oars and other crafts and scrimshaw that are great for bringing a nostalgic seaside feeling to any home.

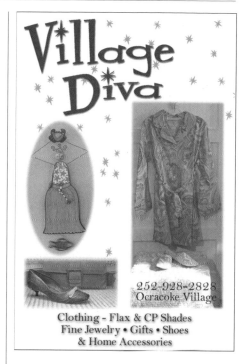

Clothing - Flax & CP Shades
Fine Jewelry • Gifts • Shoes
& Home Accessories

Sarah Searight

N.C. Hwy. 12., lower floor of Silver Lake Motel, across from South Point Seafood

Searight has exhibited her coastally inspired watercolors at several Outer Banks galleries and offers original paintings and prints. Her palette reflects the ocean, sand and sky.

See www.OcracokeGuide.com for full content, links & updates.

Ocracoke Island Trading Co.
N.C. Hwy. 12   (252) 928-7233

Men's and women's casual clothing is a highlight here. There are T-shirts galore, many name-dropped with "Ocracoke Island," in sizes ranging from small to size 3X. Sportswear, dresses, shorts, sandals and hats are also offered, as are gift and souvenir items.

Ride the Wind Surf Shop
Corner of N.C. Hwy. 12
and Silver Lake Road   (252) 928-6311

Ride the Wind is a complete watersports center offering the gear you need for surfing and kayaking (see our Recreation chapter for tour and rental information). The surf shop offers the island's best selection of swimwear and beach apparel for men and women in all the popular name brands.

Island Ragpicker
N.C. Hwy. 12   (252) 928-7571

In a great island-style "shack," the Island Ragpicker is an Ocracoke shopping tradition. It's fun to browse through room after overflowing room of goods, and you'll find it hard to leave without buying something. The Ragpicker sells its own brand of colorful rugs plus free-spirited clothing, fine T-shirts, home accessories, fine crafts, bath and body products, enlightening books, cards, music and other goods for soulful living.

island ragpicker

Artfully crafted
flotsam and jetsam . .

Open Daily • 252-928-7571

SINCE 1984

Overflowing, exciting, imaginative and whimsical!

Our own **RAGPICKER**© Rag Rugs . . .
Hand-loomed since 1973.
Finely crafted clothing and accessories for the home,
body and soul.
Tasteful t-shirts, things to use and amuse! WE ♥ Kids!
Fun stuff for them too! And . . . as always, a great book,
card and music selection.

Come in and see what's new!

10 ROOMS!

• plenty of parking •

Our customers say it best,
   "The sales crew is friendly, helpful and efficient. They make me feel at home."
   "This place goes on and on. I've never had so much fun in a shop!"
   "Our trip to Ocracoke wouldn't be the same without a visit to the ragpicker."
   "It feels and smells so good in here I don't want to leave. We can't stay away!"
   "Every time I come to the ragpicker I buy my entire year's worth of cards
      and books."
Our favorite quote by a gentleman,
   "I have as much fun in here as I do in a hardware store!"
In the "Title Wave" book room, people say,
   "I can always trust the book selection and written reviews."

**515 Irvin Garrish Hwy · on the corner of Hwy 12 and Silver Lake
P.O. Box 1713 · Ocracoke Island**

See **www.OcracokeGuide.com** for full content, links & updates.

(252) 928-3404
islandgirlnc@direcway.com
PO Box 1330, 413 Backroad, Ocracoke, NC 27960

Back Road and Sunset Drive

Island Girl
419 Back Road   (252) 928-3404

Island music will lure you into this new store on Back Road. You'll find all sorts of sea- and island-themed items such as jewelry, chimes, T-shirts, figurines, lighthouses, soaps, windsocks, sun-catchers, Old Salts figures and much more.

Java Books
Corner of Back Road and Sunset Drive, behind the Ocracoke
Coffee Co.   (252) 928-3937

Java Books is in the back of the Ocracoke Coffee Co. and has comfy, sunny chairs to sit in while you thumb through books and sip on coffee. Beach reading for the erudite, fun and literary cards and magnets, local interest books and a friendly,

helpful staff make this a worthy place to visit.

Firefly
68 Sunset Drive
(Firehouse Road) (252) 928-3401

Firefly is a treasure trove of gifts for gardeners, located on Sunset Drive, just a few doors away from the Coffee Co. Trellises, planters, birdhouses, baskets and stepping stones enhance outdoors, while lotions, soaps, books, organic dressings and candles bring the garden feeling inside. Also find items for kids, lots of plants, tools, hats and gloves.

Ocracoke Landscaping Co. & Nursery Center
109 Sunset Drive (252) 928-4703

This mostly outdoor shop sells plants and things to enhance gardens and yards, like lawn art, fountain accessories and sculptural driftwood. In the greenhouse you'll find stained glass, antique dolls, collector sports cards and some prints and paintings.

Sunflower Center
Back Road   (252) 928-6211

Plan to spend a good chunk of time at the Sunflower Center, a huge 4,000-square-foot complex housing an art gallery, a bath and body shop and a health food store. The art gallery has two levels, the first level containing primarily contemporary glass and paintings and the second level devoted to watercolors and pastels. The art is mostly by local artists, and you can find the work of five local jewelry makers here. Look for the brick garden arches out front.

Teach's Hole is as much an attraction as a place to shop. Kids love it, as will you.

Bella Fiore Pottery

80 Back Road   (252) 928-2826

Sarah Fiore's working studio showcases her vividly colored pottery. Her works are microwave, oven and dishwasher safe, including plates, bowls, mugs, sushi sets and dishes, and all have handmade glazes. The gallery also stocks all-natural bath products, ceramic art, aromatic candles, handmade jewelry, pillows and distinctive objets d'art. Think functional luxury.

Secret Garden Gallery

Back Road   (252) 928-6793

Secret Garden offers a stunning, graceful and somehow earthy collection of art, representing a number of North Carolina artists, including owner Barbara Hardy's handcrafted silver jewelry. Paintings and watercolors, photography, pottery and furniture are just some of the intriguing items found here. Occasionally the gallery mounts a show; openings are always well-attended by island art aficionados.

Ocracoke Cigar and Wine

Ocean View Road, past the Pony Island Restaurant on the left (252) 928-3021

Seek out this shop as its knowledgeable staff will help you select the perfect accompaniment for your meal or occasion. Ocracoke Cigar and Wine takes special care of its products, storing cigars in a humidor and wines on their sides in a walk-in wine refrigerator. Gifts and gadgetry for wine-lovers are sold here, as are tobacco accessories, souvenirs, soaps, oils and incense.

Down Point Lighthouse Area
(Creek, Loop and Lighthouse Roads)

Pamlico Gifts

Lighthouse Road (252) 928-6561

This is one of the remaining original Ocracoke gift shops, hidden in a residential area near the lighthouse. It's worth seeking out when you're biking or walking around the village. The shop stocks local art and crafts, shark's teeth, stained glass, ship models and other gifts. It's a block toward the water from the lighthouse, down a path on the right.

The Blue Door

49 Lighthouse Road (252) 928-7216

Here's a really cool place. This shop is chockfull of antique furniture and assorted nostalgic items, heirloom-quality quilts, funky artwork, swingy dresses, estate jewelry and many more things you'll want to take home.

Junction of School Road and N.C. Hwy. 12

Ocracoke Restoration Co.

Spencer's Market, N.C. Hwy. 12
and School Road (252) 928-2669

This is a most intriguing home-décor store. Its main contents are antique English stained-glass windows, but there are also architectural elements, like old doors and wrought-iron gate sections and shutters. The remarkable yet tasteful home accesso-

Books to Be Red and Deepwater Pottery reside in this quaint cottage.

See **www.OcracokeGuide.com** for full content, links & updates.

ries make it a great place to find the perfect wedding gift or house-warming present. The stained-glass lamps and English pine furniture are stunning.

Eleven Eleven Shades 'n Movies

Spencer's Market
N.C. Hwy. 12   (252) 928-9000

If the movies you choose to rent says something about who you are, so too do your accessories. Eleven Eleven sells premium sunglasses, including Maui Jim, Bolle and Ray Ban. Dave, the engaging owner, can also help you select a durable, stylish timepiece. The store also has an ever-expanding selection of DVDs and videos, including newer releases and many selections for kids.

Sally Newell Interiors

Spencer's Market
N.C. Hwy. 12   (252) 928-6141

Sally Newell is an ASID interior designer who offers both commercial and residential design services. In her store-front, she sells lamps, furniture and many home accessories. Sally is a font of creative ideas and can help with everything from a new bedskirt to designing your entire home. She also sells fresh flowers and plants and arranges wedding flowers.

Deepwater Pottery & Books to Be Red

Corner of N.C. Hwy. 12 and
School Road   (252) 928-3936

These two shops share space in a historic home. Deepwater Pottery sells incredible ceramic pieces, but it's also a gift shop with candles, soaps and body products, unique home and garden

accessories, and whimsical items you won't see anywhere else. Books to Be Red is small as bookstores go, but the well-chosen selection of titles makes it a literary powerhouse. Local interest, children's books, fiction, poetry, cards and journals are sold here. Plan to linger.

Natural Selections Hemp Shop

School Road   (252) 928-HEMP (4367)

Natural Selections has recently expanded its selection of quality clothing, hats, bags and accessories made from sturdy yet supple hemp and other all-natural fibers. Locals and return visitors in the know are building comfortable, timeless wardrobes. They also sell jewelry, candles and natural bath and body products.

Howard Street

Village Craftsmen

Howard Street   (252) 928-5541

Walking to Village Craftsmen is almost as much fun as visiting the store. It's down at the end of shady, historic Howard Street, about a block from the harbor. This shop, run by island natives since 1970, features exquisite traditional and contemporary crafts. You'll find musical instruments, pottery, cards, books, photographs, jewelry, paintings and a lot more.

N.C. Hwy. 12, North End

Dolphin's Cove

N.C. Hwy. 12   (252) 928-2683

Housed in a beautifully renovated historic home, Dolphin's Cove has wind chimes, ceramic artwork, pottery, stepping stones, candle holders and yard ornaments. Kids of all ages love the room devoted to stuffed animals and toys.

Pirate's Chest

Corner of N.C. Hwy. 12 and
Back Road   (252) 928-4992

We love this old-fashioned, mom-and-pop souvenir shop (not the kind of tacky chain souvenir stores you see in bigger beach areas). In the parking lot is an old boat full of shells. The variety of merchandise is astounding: T-shirts, shells and coral, gold jewelry, toys and inexpensive trinkets for kids, books, flotsam and jetsam, collectibles and more.

Teach's Hole

N.C. Hwy. 12   (252) 928-1718

Enjoy learning about Blackbeard the pirate at this pirate-themed shop and museum, in this new location as of June 2005. You'll find all the pirate-related things you can think of, including flags, jewelry, T-shirts, maps, books, costumes, toys and party supplies. There's also a pirate exhibit (see our Attractions chapter) that kids really like. 𝒞

Ocracoke Island Restaurants

Y ou'll be surprised at the number of great restaurants on this small island. Ocracoke's restaurants are locally owned and operated and as individual as their owners. There are no chain restaurants on this island.

Seafood is the top feature in nearly every local restaurant. Head down to the harbor to see the boats unloading their catches at the fish house. Much of the catch goes straight to the local restaurants. Fish, crabs, clams, shrimp and oysters are the local catches. If you're here during soft-shell crab season, never miss a chance to eat one of these delicacies. There's more to island dining than seafood, though. Fresh produce, meats and all the usual offerings are available on the island, and some establishments feature good old Southern cuisine. Breakfast is served in several local restaurants.

One thing to note: Restaurants and bars on Ocracoke only serve beer and wine. Liquor can be purchased at the local ABC Store, next to the Variety Store. Many restaurants close during the winter months. Call ahead if you're visiting in the off-season.

Silver Lake Harbor

sMacNally's Raw Bar and Grill
N.C. Hwy. 12   (252) 928-9999

sMacNally's is an entirely outdoor establishment smack on the harbor docks. Fresh seafood, cold beer and sunsets make it a happening spot to hang out. Excitement reaches a peak around 4:30 p.m. when the charter boats pull up and unload their catch. Gather around the raw bar for fresh raw or steamed seafood, including shrimp, oysters, crab legs and clams. You can also order Black Angus burgers and sandwiches off the grill. Steamed seafood clam bakes are available as takeout or delivery from Memorial Day to Labor Day. It's open daily until midnight in the warm season for lunch and dinner.

See www.OcracokeGuide.com for full content, links & updates.

caffeine is good

Ocracoke coffee CO.

Also Island Smoothies

252-928-7472
www.ocracokecoffee.com
On the Back Road, Ocracoke Island, NC

The Pelican Restaurant and Patio Bar

N.C. Hwy. 12   (252) 928-7431

The Pelican offers a cozy atmosphere in an historic 19th-century home tucked under a grove of twisting live oaks. Outside there's a lively patio where you can dine on 15-cent shrimp and beer and listen to live music. Inside it's a bit quieter. Dinner specialties include seafood, steaks and pasta.

Silver Lake Lounge

N.C. Hwy 12, across from the Jolly Roger, on the second floor of the Silver Lake Motel

A chill little bar with terrific sunset and harbor views, the Lounge is popular with locals.

Jolly Roger Pub and Marina

N.C. Hwy. 12   (252) 928-3703

If sitting right on the harbor with a drink in your hand and fresh seafood in your belly sounds good, stop here. Jolly Roger is right on the water across from Silver Lake Inn and Motel. It is completely open air, with no walls to block any of the view, so this is a prime sunset-viewing location. Casual lunches and dinners are served daily, with sandwiches, burgers, seafood and appetizers offered. Catch live music here at sunset in season.

Back Road

Ocracoke Coffee Co. & Island Smoothie

Back Road   (252) 928-7473

People from all over the island find their way to Ocracoke Coffee Co. at all hours of the day, lured by fresh-roasted coffee, espresso, tea, smoothies, bagels and baked goods. Once there you'll find it's hard to leave. Hang out for a while on the front porch or in one of the comfortable chairs in the yard under the trees. The bulletin board here is a good source for island events.

Back Porch Restaurant

Back Road   (252) 928-6401

The Back Porch is one of the island's great restaurants, providing a consistently pleasant dining experience. Fresh local seafood and produce are the stars of the menu, but hand-cut meats and poultry also shine. The menu changes seasonally to feature the freshest available ingredients. Taste combinations and presentation are always creative. A fine selection of wines

and homemade desserts is available to round out a perfect meal. Dine on the screened porch or inside. Note that this is a no smoking establishment.

North End of N.C. Hwy. 12 Main

Big Wahini's Hot Dog Stand
N.C. Hwy. 12, across from School Road

Convenient and affordable, Big Wahini's serves just what the name implies. Pop in here for hot dogs, chips and drinks from one of Ocracoke's younger entrepreneurs. Enjoy your meal on a shaded picnic table or take your sustenance to go.

Island Inn and Dining Room
Corner of N.C. Hwy. 12 and
Lighthouse Road   (252) 928-2796

The Island Inn Dining Room is an Ocracoke tradition, serving breakfast from 7 to 11 a.m. The atmosphere is like that of a country inn — open and friendly with country charm. Families are welcome, even those not staying at the inn. Breakfast can be simple eggs and bacon or an all-out feast of seafood omelets or pancakes.

Thai Moon
Spencer's Market
N.C. Hwy. 12   (252) 928-5100

Thai Moon adds a refreshing taste to the island dining scene. Hot and sour soup, spring rolls, egg rolls, satay, Pad Thai, noodles, vegetables, chicken, pork, beef and bean curd prepared with lemongrass, cilantro, chilis, lime juice and other spices are just the thing when you've had enough fried fish and crab cakes. Thai Moon does wonderful, innovative things to local

seafood. It's open for lunch and dinner. This is a take-out restaurant only.

Creekside Cafe
N.C. Hwy. 12   (252) 928-3606

This self-service outdoor café offers lunch and dinner daily in a pleasant, landscaped setting next to Dolphin's Cove. Choose from appetizers, sandwiches and pastas prepared with fresh local seafood, burgers, salads and daily quiche specials. There are kid-friendly menu items and wine and beer for adults.

Back Porch Lunchbox
N.C. Hwy. 12   (252) 928-3651

At the Lunchbox you can pick up a quick meal for the beach or take-out for the ferry ride. Or get good food — fast — and spend your time lounging at a shady picnic table or on their lawn. The outdoor space accommodates Frisbees, pets and energetic kids. Stop by the Back Porch Lunchbox, right on N.C. 12 next to the Pony Island Motel. They have sandwiches with inspired spreads, salads, baked goods, smoothies, ice cream, drinks and sweets.

The Flying Melon
N.C. Hwy. 12   (252) 928-2533

Two experienced and talented cooks have combined forces to open The Flying Melon, which serves brunch and dinner daily in a comfortable, casual dining room. A variety of local seafood, prepared both traditionally and with a touch of flash, shares menu space with fresh and flavorful pasta dishes and sandwiches. Beer and wine are available.

See **www.OcracokeGuide.com** for full content, links & updates.

Stop by Back Porch Lunchbox, right on N.C. 12 next to the Pony Island Motel.

Pony Island Restaurant

N.C. Hwy. 12   (252) 928-5701

Casual, family-friendly and traditional, Pony Island serves breakfast and dinner daily. Breakfasts are big and hearty — eggs, bacon, sausage, biscuits, pancakes, incredible hash browns and all the trimmings. Dinners include seafood, steaks, pastas and salads, and they'll even cook your day's catch if you'd like. Beer and wine are served, and desserts and a children's menu are available. Locals look forward to the nightly specials.

Capt. Ben's Restaurant

N.C. Hwy. 12   (252) 928-4741

Capt. Ben's is a family-oriented, nautical-themed restaurant serving lunch and dinner. Fresh local seafood, prime rib, pasta and chicken are prepared with

Breakfast 7 - 11   Dinner 5 - 9

PONY ISLAND
RESTAURANT
OCRACOKE, N. C.

Since 1959

Serving Island Hospitality
and
Local Seafood - Caught Daily
Steaks - Sandwiches - Salads
Fabulous Breakfast - Carry-out
OPEN 7 DAYS
252-928-5701

PO Box 610, Hwy 12
Ocracoke Island, NC 27960

See **www.OcracokeGuide.com** for full content, links & updates.

Southern style and local flair. Locals know this is the place to eat prime rib. Lunch features sandwiches, salads and Ben's delicious crab cakes. Every member of the family will find something to suit them on Capt. Ben's large and varied menu. Beer, wine, desserts and a children's menu are available.

The Fig Tree Bakery and Deli and the Sweet Tooth
N.C. Hwy. 12   (252) 928-3481

With the combination of these two businesses, all your cravings can be satisfied in one spot. Deli sandwiches are made to order, and salads, spreads and other treats like deviled eggs can be had from the deli case. The Fig Tree packs up a great to go lunch for fishing trips, beach days or ferry rides, or you can buy sliced meats and cheeses and assemble your own. Complement your meal and soothe your sweet tooth with fine chocolates, fudge, ice cream or milk shakes. Scrumptious pastries and baked goods are available, as are taffy and hard candies.

Ocracoke Station
N.C. Hwy 12   (252) 928-4031

Served from the deli counter at the gas station, Ocracoke Station offers convenient, budget-conscious satisfaction. When you're in a hurry, choose a prepared deli sandwich or sub, tub of chicken, tuna or pasta salad, hot dog, pizza slice or bowl of homemade soup. Home-style lunch specials are offered during the off-season, available to go or for eating at the cozy, conversation-friendly tables. Breakfasts of croissant sandwiches, fruit, cereal, yogurt and coffee start early. Items in the deli cases are available until close and refreshed daily. Open year-round, Ocracoke Station is also a convenience store, campground and the island's only gas station.

Sargasso Grill
N.C. Hwy 12   (252) 928-2874

This restaurant marries flavor and flair, with starters like BBQ tequila shrimp and coyote oysters. The space is intimate enough for a romantic dinner and big enough to accommodate groups and families. Dining at the bar is also an

Captain Ben's Restaurant

*The nautical antique atmosphere is both relaxing and inviting.
Fine wines, assorted beers and homemade desserts will add to your dining experience.*

SERVING LUNCH AND DINNER
11:30 - 9:00 PM

252-928-4741

Jason's Restaurant

Great Food Served in a Casual Beach Atmosphere

Pizza, Subs, Sandwiches, Salads
Steaks, Chicken, Fresh Local Seafood
SUSHI -every Tuesday evening

Carry-out Available 252-928-3434
Seasonal Hours 11:30 am to 10 pm
Located on Hwy 12 next to
Tradewinds Bait & Tackle

option. The menu features seafood as well as specialty pasta dishes, roasted duck, New Zealand rack of lamb, pork tenderloin and prime rib. Filet Oscar – beef tenderloin topped with crabmeat and Béarnaise sauce – is a real treat. Diners can also opt for traditional island fare of broiled or fried seafood.

Jason's Restaurant
N.C. Hwy. 12   (252) 928-3434

Jason's Restaurant has a lot of loyal local customers because it serves good, reasonably priced food in a casual atmosphere. It's a perfect place to wind down the day in a leisurely way, especially if you sit out on the screened porch or at the bar. Pizza, subs, sandwiches, salads, steaks, chicken and, of course, fresh seafood are served for lunch and dinner. You can count on mouth-watering homemade desserts and relax with beer and wine.

Café Atlantic
N.C. Hwy. 12   (252) 928-4861

Café Atlantic provides a mellow dining atmosphere in a beach-style building with marsh views and a gallery of local artwork. Dinner is served daily. The food here is top quality, featuring homemade soups, fresh seafood, beef, pasta, vegetarian entrees and fantastic desserts. Sunday brunch is a popular and yummy affair, with mimosas and decadent breakfast entrees, wraps, salads and sandwiches. A children's menu is available, and for adults, beer and a thoughtful wine selection. This is a nonsmoking restaurant.

See **www.OcracokeGuide.com** for full content, links & updates.

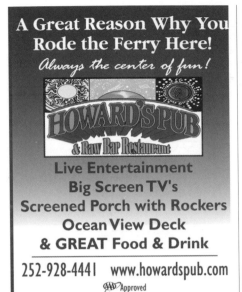
Howard's Pub and Raw Bar and Restaurant

N.C. Hwy. 12   (252) 928-4441

Howard's Pub is one of the most well-known bars and eateries on the coast of North Carolina. It seems that everybody who comes to Ocracoke goes to Howard's at least once during his or her stay. Fun-loving Howard's is famous for being open 365 days a year, even on Christmas and during hurricanes. It's open for lunch and dinner, serving the full menu until 2 a.m. during the season. Fresh local shrimp, clams, fish and live Maine lobster are highlights, but there are also steaks, ribs, subs, burgers, salads, sandwiches and pizza. More than 200 beers are served here. Sit indoors or out on the large screened porch. Enjoy live music here almost every night of the week in the summer.

Ocracoke Island Accommodations ❧

Accommodations on Ocracoke Island are individually run and therefore have a lot of character. There are no chain hotels on the island. The options range from homey bed and breakfasts to elegant inns and from mom-and-pop motels to luxurious condominium-style suites. Make your reservations well ahead of time, especially for the spring, summer and fall. Some accommodations stay open year round, but others close for the winter, so always call ahead.

Silver Lake Harbor

Anchorage Inn and Marina
Motel
N.C. Hwy. 12   (252) 928-1101
The Anchorage offers modern lodgings and resort amenities, including a marina and fishing center with charters and boat rentals available, a dock and a boat ramp, a gazebo, a private pool and sundeck and a raw bar and grill on the harbor. Shops and restaurants are just steps away. The Anchorage provides 39 motel-style rooms, most with a view of Silver Lake. Elevator access is available to the upper floors of the five-story inn. Pets are allowed in some rooms for a fee. It's open March through November.

Harborside Motel
Motel, Efficiencies
N.C. Hwy. 12   (252) 928-3111
Harborside is a quaint motel that offers 18 rooms and four efficiencies. All rooms have a TV, phone and refrigerator. Guests are welcome to use the sun deck, dock and boat ramps across the street. Complimentary breakfast is offered. The motel is within walking distance of the shops and restaurants of Ocracoke village and the ferry docks. It is open Easter through mid-November.

Joyce's of Ocracoke Waterfront Motel and Dockage

Motel, Efficiencies
N.C. Hwy. 12   (252) 928-6461

Joyce's offers six efficiency apartments with fully equipped kitchens right on the harbor. You'll get great views of ferries, fishing boats, the sunset and lighthouse from the balcony, which runs the entire length of the second floor. These modern, comfortable accommodations are above Joyce's gift shop. There is a dock for fishing and crabbing, an outdoor shower and dockage for your boat with power and water.

Bluff Shoal Motel

Motel
N.C. Hwy. 12   (252) 928-4301

Bluff Shoal Motel is small and quiet,
perfect for a simple island getaway. The seven motel-style rooms are large, with two double beds, private baths, small refrigerators, heat and air-conditioning, TVs, telephones and large windows that open to catch the breezes. You can park right at your door, and there's a long front porch for relaxing. Bluff Shoal is at the heart of the harbor activity and is open year-round.

Captain's Landing

Hotel-style Suites
N.C. Hwy. 12   (252) 928-5711

Captain's Landing has elegant waterfront suites and a penthouse overlooking Silver Lake. When staying here, you are assured a private deck and fully equipped kitchen. Suites have one bedroom and a sleeper sofa in the living room. The penthouse offers a gourmet kitchen, master suite, a guestroom, an office with a sleeper sofa, two full baths and a laundry room.

Deepwater dockage is available to guests. Reservations are made through Sandy Shores Realty at the number above.

Silver Lake Harbor Silver Lake Drive

Corinne's Studio Apartments
Efficiency Apartments
Silver Lake Drive   (252) 928-5851

Corinne's offers three studio apartments right along the harbor. The efficiency apartments feature air-conditioning and heat, cable TV, a private deck and a hot tub. Rooms are tastefully furnished and have small kitchenettes.

Pirate's Quay Condo Hotel
Hotel Suites
Silver Lake Drive   (252) 928-3002

Pirate's Quay offers six thoroughly modern, luxurious condominiums in a three-story building overlooking the harbor. The condos are rented hotel-style on a nightly basis. Each suite has two bedrooms, one and a half or two baths, a Jacuzzi, a full kitchen with dishes and cookware, a living room and dining room, maid and linen service and a private deck overlooking the harbor. Every condo accommodates six guests (up to two children). Deepwater boat dockage is available for each unit. It's open year round.

Wagon Wheel Cottages
Efficiencies
Silver Lake Drive   (252) 928-5321

These small cottages are beloved by the families, hunters and fishermen who have long rented here. Each has a full kitchen and a simple, homey interior. Right on the harbor, they've been owned and operated by the same family for more than 40 years.

The OCRACOKE HARBOR INN

Relax on your private deck and enjoy picturesque Silver Lake Harbor.

Office 252-928-5731 • Reservations 888-456-1998

16 Rooms and 7 Suites • Continental Breakfast • Boat Dockage
Jacuzzi Suites • Outdoor Grilling Area • Charter Boat & Bike Rentals

144 Silver Lake Road • www.ocracokeharborinn.com

The Ocracoke Harbor Inn

Motel
Silver Lake Drive   (252) 928-5731
or   (888) 456-1998

This aptly named inn overlooks Silver Lake harbor, with private decks off every room so no one misses the view. The inn has 16 rooms and seven suites, all tastefully decorated. The studio-style suites offer two-person whirlpool tubs and kitchenettes. Continental breakfast is complimentary. Guests have access to boat docks, outdoor showers and bikes. The inn is open year round.

The Castle on Silver Lake

Bed and Breakfast, Villas
155 Silver Lake Drive (252) 928-3505
or   (800) 471-8848

With gables galore and a steep-pitched roof, The Castle looks like a magical sandcastle sitting on the Ocracoke harbor. This bed and breakfast occupies a renovated historic structure built by Ocracoke legend Sam Jones and local craftsmen. The Castle has 11 rooms, each with a private bath. A full breakfast is served. Also on the property are 16 Courtyard Villas providing accommodations for longer stays. All Castle property guests have access to the heated pool, marina, sauna, conference room and bicycles. Villas are available year-round; the Castle B&B closes in January and February.

Lighthouse Area

The Lightkeeper's Guest House

Guest Rooms
Creek Road   (252) 928-1821

The Lightkeeper's Guest House is similar to a bed and breakfast inn in that

See www.OcracokeGuide.com for full content, links & updates.

The Castle

Rooms & Suites & Full Breakfast

A Bed & Breakfast on Silver Lake

800-471-8848
252-928-3505

Experience part of Ocracoke's history and hospitality.
PO Box 908, Silver Lake Rd. Ocracoke Island, NC 27960
E-mail: innkeeper@thecastlebb.com
www.thecastlebb.com

many separate guests rent rooms in one big house, but in this case breakfast is not served. Rather, guests can bring their own groceries and are welcome to prepare meals in the kitchen. There are five private bedrooms in this old charmer, which was built by a retiring lightkeeper in 1929. Bathrooms are shared, and there is no air conditioning. But The Lightkeeper's Guest House provides plenty of old island hospitality, especially on the numerous porches and in the parlors. The cupola room is a special treat, offering panoramic views of the village.

The Cove B&B

Bed and Breakfast
21 Loop Road   (252) 928-4192
    Off the beaten path behind the lighthouse, The Cove occupies a beautiful beach house and offers views of the

Photo Credit: Michael McOwen

The Lightkeeper's Guest House provides plenty of old island hospitality.

Lighthouse and Sound Views

The **Cove** Bed & Breakfast

21 Loop Road, PO Box 1300,
Ocracoke Island, NC 27960
252-928-4192
www.thecovebb.com
E-mail: thecovebb@beachlink.com

OSCAR'S HOUSE
built 1940
Bed and Breakfast, since 1984
A peaceful retreat for
personal and spiritual renewal.

1 block from Silver Lake, 1 mile from the Ocean
on NC Route 12 in the village

Therapeutic Massage Available
Workshops & Retreats

Ann Ehringhaus
Rt 12, PO Box 206, Ocracoke Island, NC 27960
ocracokeoscar@yahoo.com
252-928-1311

Pamlico Sound, the lighthouse and spectacular sunsets. The house is large and rambling and has two suites and four rooms, each with its own bath and balcony. The whole house can be rented for retreats or weddings. Full breakfasts are served. This is a nonsmoking inn for people older than 12. Bicycles are available. It's open year-round.

N.C.Hwy.12
(Main Highway North End)

Island Inn and Dining Room
Motel, Condominiums N.C. Hwy. 12 and Lighthouse Road   (252) 928-4351
    Built in 1901, the building that houses the Island Inn is an Ocracoke icon, having served as a lodge, school, private residence and naval headquarters. The Island Inn offers the ambiance of a country inn, with

35 rooms and a legendary restaurant on site. The main building houses individual rooms and suites, all furnished with antiques and quilts. There are adults-only rooms and suites as well. The inn has a large swimming pool and covered decks with rockers. Across the street are the Island Inn Villas, 19 condominium-style luxury units. The inn is open year round.

Oscar's House B&B
Bed and Breakfast
N.C. Hwy. 12   (252) 928-1311
    Oscar's House B&B occupies a 1940 house built by Captain Burrus, the Lighthouse Keeper. Now a gem of an inn, Oscar's House has four guestrooms and a delightful innkeeper, Ann Ehringhaus, who is a photographer, author and massage therapist. Ann offers a peaceful setting for personal renewal, with massage therapy plus various workshops and

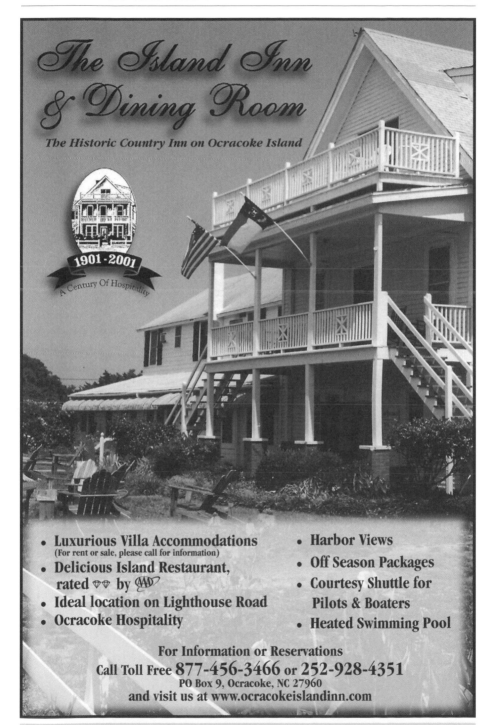

The Island Inn & Dining Room

The Historic Country Inn on Ocracoke Island

1901 - 2001
A Century Of Hospitality

- **Luxurious Villa Accommodations**
  (For rent or sale, please call for information)
- **Delicious Island Restaurant,** rated ◊◊ by AAA
- **Ideal location on Lighthouse Road**
- **Ocracoke Hospitality**

- **Harbor Views**
- **Off Season Packages**
- **Courtesy Shuttle for** Pilots & Boaters
- **Heated Swimming Pool**

For Information or Reservations
Call Toll Free **877-456-3466** or **252-928-4351**
PO Box 9, Ocracoke, NC 27960
and visit us at www.ocracokeislandinn.com

See www.OcracokeGuide.com for full content, links & updates.

retreats. There are only two bathrooms for
guests, so sharing is essential. Complimentary full breakfasts are served. The inn is
within walking distance of all the village
activity and is open from April through
October.

Thurston House Inn
Bed and Breakfast
N.C. Hwy. 12   (252)928-6037

This bed and breakfast inn occupies
two buildings - a 1920s island home that is
on the National Register of Historic Places
in North Carolina and a newer adjacent
building built in 1999. Decorated in
charming island style, the inn offers nine
rooms, each with a private bath, queen- or
king-size bed and cable TV. Continental
breakfasts are provided. Decks and porches
are perfect places for relaxing. The inn is
open year round.

Pony Island Motel
Hotel, Efficiencies, Suites
N.C. Hwy. 12   (252) 928-4411

Open for more than 25 years, Pony
Island is a family-owned, family-oriented
motel. It offers 50 units, including motel-
style rooms, efficiencies and suites, all
furnished in traditional island décor. Some
rooms have kitchen conveniences. Bike
rentals, boat dockage and a swimming pool
are available, and the motel is within
walking distance of island attractions. The
popular Pony Island Restaurant is next
door for breakfast and dinner. Pony Island
also operates five cottages that accommodate up to six people. The motel is open
year round.

Pelican Lodge and Pelican Lodge East B&Bs

Motel, Bed and Breakfast
Pelican Lodge: 27 Sunset Drive
Pelican Lodge East: 1021 N.C. Hwy. 12
(252) 928-1661

Owned by the same family, these two bed and breakfast lodges are about a half-mile apart. The older, less expensive Pelican Lodge is off the main road, near the firehouse and Ocracoke Coffee Co. It has four rooms with full-size beds and private baths. The new building, on the main road next to the Fig Tree Bakery, has five rooms, including one suite, with queen-size beds and private baths. A full, sit-down breakfast is served at both lodges every morning, and bikes are available to guests. The Lodge is open year round.

Back Road & Sunset Drive

Beach House B&B

Bed and Breakfast
N.C. Hwy. 12   (252) 928-1411

In an 80-year-old home furnished with antiques and collectibles, this bed and breakfast inn evokes a mood of days gone by. Guests often relax on the porch, just like in the old days. Each of the three guestrooms here has a private bath. Beach House is on N.C. 12 on the northern end of town near Howard's Pub, the airport and the beach. The owner is a former restaurateur, and breakfasts are a real treat. This is a nonsmoking establishment. Beach House is open year round.

Crews Inn B&B

Bed and Breakfast
Back Road   (252) 928-7011

Crews Inn offers a true Ocracoke Island experience in a secluded 1908 island home down an oyster-shell driveway. Five guestrooms are offered, three with a private bath and two that share a bath. The top-floor room, the Captain's Quarters, has a claw-foot tub and small deck. A continental breakfast is served on the wrap-around porch. This is a nonsmoking inn. It is open year round.

Ocracoke Cabanas

Apartments
Sunset Drive   (252) 928-6261

These four one-bedroom apartments are great for couples. Each unit offers a whirlpool tub, fireplace, full kitchen, washer & dryer, TV, VCR and CD player. There is a pool and outdoor shower, and guests have access to bikes. Quiet and secluded, Ocracoke Cabanas are only a short walk away from the Coffee Co., fine dining and the activity around the harbor.

Blackbeard's Lodge

Motel, Efficiencies
Back Road   (252) 928-3421
                        or (800) 892-5314

Blackbeard's is the one of the oldest motels on Ocracoke, and it's legendary, just like its namesake. The rambling lodge has 37 units, with accommodations to suit any need, whether it's a simple motel-style room or an efficiency apartment sleeping eight and providing a full kitchen and dining room. All rooms have cable TV, and most any amenity you could need is available in at least one room. Blackbeard's is family-oriented, with a heated pool, game room, pool tables, bicycles, a fish-cleaning station and a large porch with rockers. It's open year round.

Edward's of Ocracoke

Motel, Efficiencies, Cottages
Back Road   (252) 928-4801
                        or (800) 254-1359

Edward's offers relaxed accommodations to suit any traveler's need — eight motel rooms, three efficiencies, six apartment cottages and two private cottages. The accommodations are simple, affordable and perfect for the fishing-village lifestyle of Ocracoke. Most of the units have screened porches. Pets are allowed in some of the cottages for an extra charge. Edward's is open from mid-March until New Year's Day.

Sand Dollar Motel

Motel, Efficiency
Sand Dollar Lane   (252) 928-5571

This quiet motel is tucked away near The Back Porch Restaurant. It offers 11 rooms, an efficiency apartment and a two-bedroom cottage. There's a secluded pool on site, and guests are treated to a complimentary continental breakfast. It's open from April through November.

Vacation Rentals

Sometimes you want – or need – more space and amenities than you get with a hotel room. Ocracoke Island is rich with rentable houses and cottages for just this purpose. Prices vary depending on location, amenities and size, but you'll have no trouble finding something to suit your needs.

Ocracoke Island Realty

N.C. Hwy. 12

north end of town   (252) 928-6261

Ocracoke Island Realty offers more than 150 rental properties, ranging from charming historic cottages to elegant new homes. Vacation rentals are offered at various locations throughout the island. The company also handles real estate sales. Call for a free rental brochure that details

each and every property.

Sandy Shores Realty
N.C. Hwy. 12

north end of town   (252) 928-5711

Sandy Shores Realty offers more than 135 vacation homes and accommodations for rent throughout the island. Accommodations, ranging from simple to luxurious, are individually owned and reflect the tastes of the owners. This company also handles real estate sales. Call for a detailed rental brochure.

Campgrounds

Ocracoke Campground – National Park Service
N.C. Hwy. 12   (252) 928-5111
or (800) 365-CAMP

The National Park Service's Ocracoke Campground is on the oceanfront about 3 miles from Ocracoke Village. It's tucked behind a row of dunes, beyond which lies the wide, unspoiled Ocracoke beach. The campground is suitable for tents and RVs and offers parking at each site, running water, flush toilets, cold showers, a dump station and charcoal grills. There are very few trees here and, therefore, no shade. The facility is open from spring through fall. Bring mosquito repellent in the summer. Pets are allowed on leashes. Reservations are recommended.

Beachcomber Campground
N.C. Hwy. 12   (252) 928-4031

Behind Ocracoke Station, this campground has 29 tent sites with electricity and water hookups and seven tent sites. Hot showers and full bathrooms are available, as are picnic tables and grills. Pets are allowed on leashes. It's open from late March through November. Reservations are recommended.

Teeter's Campground
British Cemetery Rd.   (252) 928-3135

Teeter's is tucked into the trees down British Cemetery Road, near the heart of the village. It offers two full hookup sites, 12 sites with electricity and water hookup and 10 tent sites. Hot showers, grills and picnic tables are available. It's open March through November. Reservations are recommended. 𝒞

Photo Credit: Michael McOwen

See **www.OcracokeGuide.com** for full content, links & updates.

Beulah and Clenon Boyette at the desk of the Boyette House Hotel in the 1960s.

See **www.OcracokeGuide.com** for full content, links & updates.

Ocracoke Island

Here at the edge
enveloped by wind
encirled by stars
where scallop and olive shell
at our bare feet proclaim divinity,
here is where we have emigrated.

East is tidal, effusive, amorphous.
Wet.

Macadam and steel stretch forever out there
in that sharp vertical domain.
The rigid black accoutrements
of a gray confined civility.

There are lines of demarcation.

Feather and bone and clam are here
Green wave, white spray, blue fin.
We are all salt tinged,
Such is our commonality

Here at the edge
of sand and sea
in our weathered principality.

carmie prete

Photo by ann ehringhaus